Walking in the Supernatural Power of Prayer

Praying from the Heavenlies to Receive Victory on the Earth

H.A. Lewis
Patricia Lewis

Walking in the Supernatural Power of Prayer

Praying from the Heavenlies to Receive Victory on the Earth

ISBN: 978-0-9988129-0-8 Soft cover

Copyright © 2017 by Joshua International dba H.A.Lewis Ministries

All rights reserved. No part of this book may be reproduced or transmitted in any form or by any means, electronic or mechanical, including photocopying, recording, or by any information storage and retrieval system, without permission in writing from the copyright owner.

This book was printed in the United States of America.

Walking in the Supernatural Power of Prayer

Stand UP, Gear UP, Move Forward in prayer

**Spiritual Warfare Extreme
Series**

**H.A. Lewis
Patricia Lewis**

Heaven Waits on YOU for the Earth to Move

"There must be a move on earth before there is a move in heaven. It is not heaven that binds first but the earth. It is not heaven that looses first but the earth."
Ref: *Watchmen Nee, "The Prayer Ministry of the Church,"*

When Heaven is silent and God is not moving mightily it always comes down to a failure on the earth and in the church to pray!

Unseen to the natural eye, angels engage in battle in the spiritual world from the third heaven where ALL authority abides

Individually or collectively as we pray, they may guide the governments of the earth as well as events in our own personal lives which take place from the second heaven.

Our means of praying must be ABOVE the second heavens using the mind of Christ as we are seated with him in heavenly realms..

[Ephesians 2:6] And God raised us up with Christ and seated us with him in the heavenly realms in Christ Jesus

We must have Him. Let our cry and effort be heavenward, until the windows are opened and the fullness of His glory manifested."

ONLY Through Corporate Prayer are we Given the Promise of Jesus' Manifest Presence

* The power of being "gathered in Jesus' name" rather than just coming to church
* [**Matt. 18:20**] [Amplified]

The church of Jesus Christ [Yeshua] needs to shift the focus from trying to figure out how to attract people, to seeking to attract God's presence and His power to our gatherings

Be a FRIEND of GOD
PRAY

John 15:15

I no longer call you servants, because a servant does not know his master's business. Instead, I have called you friends, for everything that I learned from my Father I have made known to you.

WE ARE HIS EARS

We are His tabernacles here on earth

Our ideas come to life when inspired by the Holy Spirit.
The Holy Spirit speaks through supernatural wisdom.
When the Holy Spirit SPEAKS, its time to LISTEN and come into agreement
With what is shared.

WE ARE HIS MOUTH

Then we SPEAK it into existence so HIS will can be manifested
[Proverbs 8:21]

Table of Contents

Introduction: 11

Chapter 1:   13
I Stand at the Door and Knock – The Invitation

Chapter 2:   19
Understanding the Marriage Covenant

Chapter 3:   24
Communion with God – The Tabernacle Experience
   Part 1: Living the Tabernacle Experience
   Part 2: Learning to Live the Tabernacle Experience

Chapter 4:   28
Communion with God – The Voice of God
   Part 1: Becoming Still to Know His Voice
   Part 2: Living Out of the Voice of God
   Part 3: Journaling – A Means of Discerning God's Voice

Chapter 5:   35
The Keys of Favor, Grace and Mercy

Chapter 6:   37
Abiding in Christ

Chapter 7:   40
Christ's Identity in Me

Chapter 8:   51
Who I Am in God

Chapter 9:   54
The Holy Spirit vs. The Spirit of Christ

Chapter 10:   57
Praying From the Third Heaven
Heaven Waits On YOU for Earth to Move

Chapter 11: 64
My Consecration as a Christian

Chapter 12: 67
What Obedience Produces

Chapter 13: 70
The Authority Abiding in Us
~ Praying in Jesus Name

Chapter 14: 76
Prayer Warfare is Spiritual Warfare

Chapter 15: 78
Prayer Facts

Chapter 16: 81
Foundations of Prayer

Chapter 17: 83
Supernatural Power of Prayer

Chapter 18: 87
Endurance in Prayer UNTIL the Answer comes

Chapter 19: 90
Dismantling the Enemy's Activity

Chapter 20: 93
Biblical Examples of Powerful Prayer

Chapter 21: 96
Inviting the Holy Spirit to be Our Guide in Prayer

Chapter 22: 99
Praying For Your Town, City, And Country

Chapter 23: 107
Encourage Yourself Confessions

Chapter 24: 117
Men Who Met God – Forefathers of Faith and Prayer

CONSECRATE YOUR MARRIAGE RELATIONSHIP
Biblical Meaning: the separation of oneself from things that are unclean.

[Joel 2:15-17] NASB
Blow a trumpet in Zion, **consecrate a fast**, proclaim a solemn assembly, gather the people, sanctify the congregation, assemble the elders, gather the children and nursing infants. Let the bridegroom come out of his room and the bride out of her bridal chamber. Let the priests, the Lord's ministers, weep between the porch and the altar, and let them say, "Spare Your people, O Lord, and do not make Your inheritance a reproach, a by word among the nations. Why should they among the peoples say, "Where is their God?"

[Joshua 3:5] NIV
Joshua told the people, "**Consecrate** yourselves, for tomorrow the Lord will do amazing things among you."

[Joshua 3:5] NLT
Then Joshua told the people, "**Purify** yourselves, for tomorrow the Lord will do great wonders among you."

[2 Chronicles] 7:14 KJV
If my people, which are called by my name, shall humble themselves, and pray, and seek my face, and turn from their wicked ways; then will I hear from heaven, and will forgive their sin, and will heal their land.

Walking in the Supernatural Power of Prayer

Introduction

For most people today praying only happens when there is an emergency or something bad has happened. In fact whether they know Christ or not they will use the cliché, "I'll be praying for you", as some form of comfort to the one going through a difficult time. Does that mean praying is useless? Why pray?

Any person that believes and adheres to a deity prays. Those who follow after false gods are very disciplined in their prayers or chants. Sadly all their energy produces nothing. However, as believers in the Lord Jesus Christ, we should be the most disciplined in our prayers. Why? We are praying to the one True God after all.

Sadly we haven't fully grasped the truth of what prayer is and the power it produces; not only in our circumstances and the circumstances around us, but within our very own lives. Since it is so vitally important in our daily walk with Christ, what exactly is prayer?

Prayer is simply communicating or fellowshipping with God. It is like a conversation between intimate friends. There is that level of respect, love, joy, and fulfillment when given the privilege to speak with the God of Abraham, Isaac, and Jacob.

Jesus Christ became the propitiation for our sins and opened up the way so that we are able to have those intimate conversations with our Creator. In [**Luke 18:1**] Jesus told us that we ought always to pray and not to faint. He is telling us that He wants us to spend more time in prayer so He can tell us how much He loves us.

Prayer **IS**:
- Our personal connection with God
- Spending time with Him that brings results like: learning His wisdom, drawing strength, being filled with His quietness or peace basking in His love and trusting him.
- Powerful, energizing, dynamic and revitalizes the one who prays
- For changing situations, circumstances, and people's hearts

Prayer **IS NOT**:
- Reciting words
- Just saying prayers to gets results is not true prayer
- For the purpose of changing God

The power of prayer stands when all other powers fail. World systems change, ideologies change, balances of economics change; however, the power of prayer available to you will never fail. It cannot be defeated.

Five Keys to Powerful Prayer
A Deep Relationship with God

A clean heart [**Psalms 51:10**]
Praying the word [**Isaiah 55:11**]
Praying in faith believing [**Matthew 21:22**]
Spirit led praying [**Colossians 1:9-14**]

so is my word that goes out from my mouth:
It will **not** return to me empty,
but will **accomplish** what I desire
and **achieve** the purpose for **which I sent it.** [**Isaiah 55:11**]

If you believe, you will receive whatever you ask for in prayer."
[**Matthew 21:22**]

Chapter 1
I Stand at the Door and Knock – The Invitation

>>The Invitation to the Marriage<<
Behold I stand at the door and knock

The Beginning of Intimacy
Here I am! I stand at the door and knock. If anyone hears my voice and opens the door, I will come in and eat with that person, and they with me. [Revelation 3:20] NIV

The significance of this is that we have a choice and OUR WILL is ours. It's exactly the same as the ancient Hebrew bride who could choose to either ask her father to *open the door*, or *leave it shut*. If she refuses to allow her father to open the door, the groom and his father then leave the threshold and return home. The application for the church is that God the Father, as the Father of the groom (Jesus) made the arrangements and paid the bride price – the Blood of His Son, Jesus.

Ephesians 5:25b *…Christ loved the church and gave Himself up for her.*
John 3:16 *For God so loved the world that He gave His one and only Son, that whoever believes in Him shall not perish but have eternal life*

Giving up the Son and shedding the blood of the Son paid the bride price. The marriage arrangement was sealed with the groom's (Jesus') blood.

If the prospective Hebrew bride agrees and her father opens the door, then the initial agreement to be married would be worked out through intense and animated discussions. Then it would be formalized in a written contract called *Ketubah*.

The prospective bride was the *only one* who could back out of this agreement right up until the very instant of the marriage being consummated and she does not need any special reason. On the other hand, once the initial proposal has been made and accepted, the groom was **totally committed** and only by a *writ of divorce* on extremely limited grounds could he ever back out. If he died before the marriage was consummated, she inherited his estate.

Biblical Marriage consists of four types of covenant beginning with the Jewish betrothal process

Servanthood ⇒ Blood Covenant
Friendship ⇒ Salt Covenant
Inheritance ⇒ Sandal Covenant
Praise ⇒ Sealed Covenant

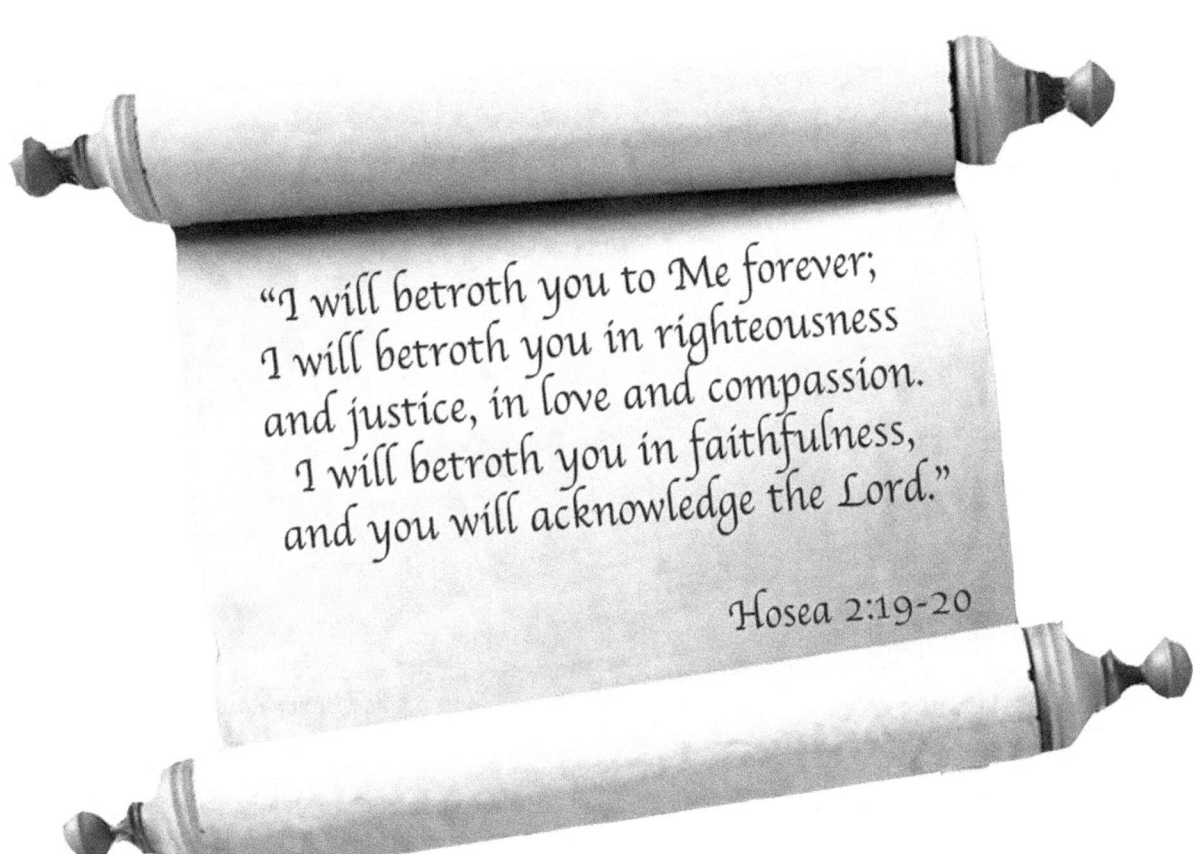

Walking in the Supernatural Power of Prayer

♦The First Cup of Wine – Blood Covenant♦
The Period of Betrothal

After we have accepted Jesus as Lord, He asks us if we will enter into the <u>covenant of betrothal</u> with Him by walking in a loving relationship with Him as the bridegroom. **During this process** the **first** cup of wine that is drunk between the bride to be and the groom to be and there families corresponds to the ***blood covenant***, which represents the very beginning of a committed surface relationship known as "being saved."

The first cup represents *sanctification* and was a symbol of a servant the blood covenant between the two families. This cup was consumed as soon as the door was closed. This indicated that both families would serve each other, thereby strengthening the families. Sanctification embodies the idea of setting aside our lives to serve God. This is the time of preparation where the bride is prepared and trained to take on the role of a wife.

♦The Second Cup of Wine – Salt Covenant♦

The **second** cup of wine drunk by the bride to be, the groom to be and their families corresponded to the salt covenant and represented to the friendship level in the betrothal process. This is the deeper commitment by which time both the bride to be, the groom to be, and their family members have essentially pledged eternal bonds to each other.

The **second** cup was also the cup of bargaining representing the salt covenant which is an eternal covenant between the families. Everyone present drank the cup. The two families were working to become eternal friends. It is at this time that the betrothal could fall part. If they made it through this process, then the marriage would stand a chance to come to pass.

♦ The Third Cup of Wine – Sandal Covenant♦
Total Commitment

The **third** cup drunk by the bride to be and the groom to be is seen in the Last Supper. This covenant represents **total commitment** between the bride and groom and the inheritance level. At this point during the ancient Hebrew betrothal process, the couples are sealed to each other. If one of them should die before the wedding, the other person would still inherit everything from the person who died.

The third cup is also known as the cup of redemption or inheritance. This cup is to drunk at the end of the meal by the bride to be and groom to symbolize their exclusive commitment to each other. The engagement is considered sealed. Now the scribes could come in and draw up the marriage contract called a **Ketubah.**

♦The Fourth Cup of Wine – Cup of Praise and Celebration♦

The **fourth** and **final** cup drunk by the bride and groom signify their final coming together in a state of **eternal unity**. This fourth cup, which is drank by the bride and groom at their wedding, is the cup we will drink at the **marriage supper of the lamb**. We become eligible for the **fourth** covenant after we have met the requirements of the three previous covenants.

**Please Note: We are saved by grace and NOT by the law.

1 Peter 2:9 But you are a chosen people, a royal priesthood, a holy nation, God's special possession, that you may declare the praises of him who called you out of darkness into his wonderful light.

NOTES

Chapter 2
Understanding the Marriage Covenant

Unhindered Prayer begins with a Marriage Covenant Relationship

In today's society, the Biblical meaning of the word *marriage* is truly disappearing. When we look in God's word we find that *marriage* actually means *covenant*. This applies not only to our spouses but also to our God and Savior. When my wife and I said our vows, it was meaningful with commitment. We serve and love each other unconditionally as Christ does for everyone.

Marriage was conceived in the Bible. It was conceived in the heart of God and there, too, we find the key to a successful marriage. The Bible attaches great importance to marriage — much more, I think, than most churchgoers or Christians realize.

A **marriage covenant** demands commitment — total, unreserved, whole-hearted commitment. Marriage is not an experimental relationship. It is not a trial. It can only succeed on the basis of total commitment. In a **covenant**, God sets the terms for a commitment. Man does not set the terms. The problem with Israel in the **days of Malachi** is that they were trying to set their terms for how marriage should be and God said," I won't accept that."

>>It began with marriage and it will end with marriage.<<

Human history, according to the Bible, *began with a marriage*. God created Adam and then He said it was not good for Adam to be alone, and God Himself formed and brought to him a wife, a helpmeet. Marriage initiated in the heart of God, not in the thought of man, and I believe once we get away from God's concept of marriage, it's not going to work.

Furthermore, the Bible *ends with marriage*. The great climax of all human history is the **marriage supper** of the Lamb. Since the Bible places such a tremendous importance on marriage, my question is: do we see that our marriage relationship with Christ resembles the marriage relationship with our spouse? What type of relationship do we have and is our flesh still in control, wanting what we want and how we want it and when we want it? Have we been crucified with Christ?

[**Galatians 2:20**] *I have been crucified with Christ and I no longer live, but Christ lives in me. The life I now live in the body, I live by faith in the Son of God, who loved me and gave himself for me.*
 √ If we applied this verse in our marriage to our spouses, there would be **NO** divorce.
 √ This verse should also be applied to our marriage with Christ.

I believe that the Bible is a true, relevant, and an up-to-date book. I believe it has the answers to life's problems today. I believe all we need to do is apply it and it works. For me, it will be 44 years of marriage with my wife. It was not easy at times because the will and emotions want what it wants. However, as we lean on Christ and the Holy Spirit then we'll see what needs to be changed in us before we cast a stone against our partner. Then, when we pray for them, we will be successful because we are doing it out of a clean heart.

[**Matthew 7:3-5**] NIV *Why do you look at the speck of sawdust in your brother's eye and pay no attention to the plank in your own eye? How can you say to your brother, 'Let me take the speck out of your eye,' when all the time there is a plank in your own eye? You hypocrite, first take the plank out of your own eye, and then you will see clearly to remove the speck from your brother's eye.*

In **Ephesians 5**, Paul has been speaking about marriage. He compares the relationship of Jesus Christ and His church to that of a bridegroom to His bride. He concludes this comparison with this statement, "This is a great mystery." One of the modern translations says, "*a profound mystery.*" He is speaking about **marriage**.

Now we need to understand that in the language of the New Testament, the word "*mystery*" had a specific meaning. It meant a secret that most people didn't know but that could be learned if you went through a process of "*initiation*" and got in with the right group. And so, that's what marriage is. It's a "*secret*" that most people don't know but it can be learned if you go through the process of "*initiation*".

The Key to a Successful Marriage
The secret is that relationship is communication.

In the book of **Malachi** we read that Israel as a nation was NOT very close to God. God had given them His law BUT, in most cases, they had been somewhat disobedient and, as a result, they were NOT enjoying the blessings that God had promised them. They had a lot of problems and some of their problems were like the problems of many people today. And God puts His finger on the reason for their problems. It's in [**Malachi 2:13–14**] *Another thing you do: You flood the Lord's altar with tears. You weep and wail because he no longer looks with favor on your offerings or accepts them with pleasure from your hands. You ask, "Why?" It is because the Lord is the witness between you and the wife of your youth. You have been unfaithful to her, though she is your partner, the wife of your marriage covenant.*

Do we understand that they were religious people and **not relational**? They were doing a lot of praying but God wasn't answering their prayers. And they said, "For what reason?" Then the Lord gives them His answer. Daily He and our angels are witnessing us in our physical marriage to our spouses BUT also to our spiritual union with HIM. In our disconnection, we lose favor.

>Three Points to Notice<

♦**First**: religion does not necessarily produce successful marriages or a happy home. These people were very religious. They were praying all the time they were in the temple, but their homes were in a mess. There was no Biblical order. Let's bear that in mind.

♦**Second:** a wrong relationship between a husband and wife hinders a relationship with God. God said He wouldn't hear their prayers and they said, "Why?" and He said to them, "Because you haven't dealt right with your wife. You've been unfaithful to the wife of your covenant."

In **1 Peter 3**, Peter instructs husbands to be careful how they live with their wives so that their prayers will not be hindered. In other words, if you pray out of an unhappy marriage, and it is not an ordered home, your prayer may not be very effective. God says to get your home in order.

♦ **Third: Vital point** — it is the key to the successful marriage. It is the last word of that Scripture, the word *covenant*. It is the realization, out of Scripture, that marriage is a *covenant*. **Covenant** is one of the key concepts of the Bible. The same word that is translated *covenant* is also translated **testament**. The whole Bible comes to us in the form of *two covenants or two testaments*. Absolutely amazing! His written word comes to us in the form of a *covenant*.

A covenant is called a *b'rit* in Hebrew. It defines an ongoing relationship with *no appointed end*. It is a commitment to develop a continuing relationship and its existence implies interaction between partners that is a dynamic and growing process.

The Holy Spirit today is seeking the entire earth for the **Bride of Christ**. In the Old Testament Abraham is a type of the heavenly **Father**. He sends his servant, Eliezer, a type of the **Holy Spirit** to find a wife for Isaac, a type of the **Son**. And Rebecca, the wife found for Isaac is a type of the church.

What do the Scriptures mean when they talk about the church being the **Bride of Christ**? In the Old Testament many references are made where God speaks of Israel as His *wife*. And many times He is pointing out her unfaithfulness and her adultery with the gods of the surrounding nations, which is happening today.

God still yearns for our return to Him. He doesn't *divorce* us; however, we remain separated from the fullness of Him, His presence, and His blessings. His continued call and His desire, by the courting of the Holy Spirit, is His hope for us to be lovers again in a much deeper relationship.

His coming is near. His desire is to bring heaven to the earth and to bestow His blessings and miracles. He is looking for a bride without blemish [**Ephesians 5:27**] and holy and blameless. His heart's desire is for us to come into the *inner court*.

For many years we have been comfortable with just being saved and hanging in the *outer court*. We are not walking in the fullness of His word. We show no maturity and therefore we are not good examples of His grace. However, when we are mature in the fullness of His word, we become a *friend* of God. In essence we become his favorites and we *carry his favor*.

We must move forward in this relationship of commitment. We must *trust Him*, and in return He desires to *trust us*. Why? Because there is much He desires for us to do, which will truly change those around us. Beginning in **Genesis** and continuing throughout the Old Testament, we find a record of legally binding agreements called *covenants* between God and His people, which are the basis from which all the relationships with God are built and maintained.

>>The Bible contains the greatest love story ever written.<<

God describes His people, Israel as His bride and Himself as her Husband. Within the Holy Scriptures the marriage relationship is central to everything God ordained despite recent legislation in many countries around the world. God will not be mocked; He will uphold the sanctity of marriage.

The **marriage covenant** is so significant that the Bible begins and ends with a wedding. And Jesus began His adult ministry at a wedding.

In the scriptures there are many references to the marriage covenant. We read of God referring to Himself as the Bridegroom or Husband and comparing all those who enter into covenant with Him as "the bride."

Walking in the Supernatural Power of Prayer

[Isaiah 61:10 NIV]
*I delight greatly in the Lord;
my soul rejoices in my God.
For he has clothed me with garments of salvation
and arrayed me in a robe of his righteousness,
as a bridegroom adorns his head like a priest,
and as a bride adorns herself with her jewels.*

In the **Mishnah**, Rabbinic tradition tells us that when God presented Eve to Adam, He adorned her as a bride with beautiful jewels. Then in the Garden of Eden the first wedding took place in the presence of God and witnessed by the archangel, Gabriel and Michael.
[**Genesis 2:18-25**] NIV

The LORD appeared to us in the past, saying:

"I have loved you with an everlasting love;
I have drawn you with unfailing kindness."
[**Jeremiah 31:3**]

Recommended reading:
The Two Covenants and the Second Blessing by Andrew Murray

NOTES

Chapter 3
Communion With God – The Tabernacle Experience

Part One: Living the Tabernacle Experience

Looking at the tabernacle Moses was instructed to construct, we find that, spiritually speaking, it is relevant for us today because it is the pathway into His presence. In **Exodus 25-30** we find where God gave the design of the tabernacle to Moses. In **Hebrews 8:5** we find that the design of the tabernacle given to Moses was a copy, a shadow, and a pattern of the heavenlies. The tabernacle established a 'pathway into His presence'. By adhering to the precise requirements needed in the tabernacle, humans could approach Him and hear His voice.

Today because of Christ's work on the cross, we are now considered God's tabernacle. Therefore, we can correlate the body, soul, and spirit of man with it. Moses' tabernacle had an outer court which corresponds with our body. And the body is where we receive our sense knowledge. The Holy Place corresponds with our soul. The Holy Place was illuminated by the lamp stand, and within us the Holy Spirit reveals truth to our minds. Finally there was the Holy of Holies. This corresponds to our spirit, and it is where the Shekinah glory lights our innermost being and gives us direct revelation within our hearts.

⇒**There are six pieces of furniture which represent an experience in our approach to God's presence.**⇐

- The Brazen Altar [**Exodus 27:1-8**] – THE CROSS: *This is an absolute pre-requisite to approaching God.* It is where we make the commitment to make Jesus Lord of our lives. And it is where we present our bodies as a living sacrifice unto God [**Romans 12:1, 2**]

- The Bronze Laver [**Exodus 30:17-21**] – GOD'S WORD: This is where we wash ourselves by applying the 'logos' to our lives. The applied 'logos' has a cleansing affect on us.

- The Table of Shewbread [**Exodus 25:17-21**] – THE WILL: As flour is ground fine for the making of the bread, so is our will ground fine as we totally commit our way unto the Lord.

- The Seven-Branched Golden Lampstand [**Exodus 25:31-39**] – ILLUMINED MIND: God illuminates to 'rhema' as we study and meditate on Him and His 'logos'.

- The Altar of Incense [**Exodus 30:1-10**] – EMOTIONS: Through the offering up of a continuous sacrifice of praise, our emotions are brought under the control of the Holy Spirit.

- The Ark of the Covenant [**Exodus 25:10-22**] – DIRECT REVELATION OF THE SPIRIT into our hearts: Out of worship and stillness we enter heart-to-heart communion with God. God's shekinah glory fills our hearts.

Walking in the Supernatural Power of Prayer

 **Part Two: Learning to Live the Tabernacle Experience**

When we learn to live the tabernacle way, we find a place of oneness with Almighty God. Let's make every aspect personal:

- ♦ At the brazen altar – I am a living sacrifice.
- ♦ At the bronze laver – I have washed myself by applying the Word of God.
- ♦ At the table of shewbread – My will is ground before God.
- ♦ At the golden lampstand – God illumines my mind and grants me revelation.
- ♦ At the ark of the covenant – I have learned to walk into His immediate presence in silence and receive His words spoken into my heart

According to Exodus, the altar of incense is the only tabernacle piece that had two rings for it to be carried. This goes along with the marrying of our spirit with the Spirit of God. This golden altar of incense is a place of intimacy. It is a place of oneness in prayer, praise, worship, and intercession. Here is where we become one with God and are ushered into His presence and throne room.

- ♦ At the ark of the covenant – I have learned to walk into His immediate presence in silence and receive His words spoken into my heart.

As we learn to live the tabernacle experience we are essentially learning God's voice. We begin by 'rough tuning' ourselves to God's voice [**Hebrews 12:1-3**]. We do this by finding a quiet place and silence our spirits by fixing our eyes on Jesus [**Hebrews 12:2**]. Then we facilitate the flow by writing it down. Next we must do some 'fine tuning' by removing inner blocks [**Hebrews 10:22**]. We approach God in full faith. Our hearts are sincere, honest, and committed. We harbor no reservations. Our consciences have been cleared through receiving Christ's cleansing and we have been obedient to previous *rhema* [God's spoken word].

>>Living out of the Rhema<<
- •We overcome all evil by living out of the rhema God has spoken to us.
- •We confess it with our mouths.
- •We consider other ways to stimulate others to walk in the rhema God has given them.
- •We come together with others for mutual encouragement.

>>Validating our Rhema<<
- We validate our rhema by submitting to our spiritual authority [**Hebrews 13:17**].
- We are submitted to a spiritual elder, and he/she is willing for us to bring major decisions to him/her.
- We submit our major leadings to him/her that may have a major consequence in time and/or money.

The rhema helps in restoring our spirit as we move from the body/soul to the spirit [**James 4:5**]. Just as our bodies need to eat, drink, and breathe so does our spirit. The spirit's food is digesting (meditating) the logos [**Joshua 1:8**]. The spirit's water is praying in the spirit [**John 7:38, 39; 1 Corinthians 14:2, 4, 15**]. And the spirit's breath is the rhema of the spirit [**John 6:63; Proverbs 20:27**]

NOTES

Chapter 4
Communion With God – The Voice of God

 **Part One: Becoming Still to Know His Voice**

One of the greatest challenges for the modern day Christian is to learn to be still or to silence his/herself. We must learn how to do this because scripture commands it [**Psalm 46:10**]. How can we commune with God if we don't first become still? Habakkuk went to his guard post to pray [**Habakkuk 2:1**] and Jesus went to a lonely place to pray [**Mark 1:35**].

In order for our inner man to commune with God, we must first remove external distractions. Like Habakkuk and Jesus find a place where you can be alone and undisturbed. It must be a place of no distraction by external circumstances. Secondly, we must learn to quiet our inner being. Quiet all the voices and thoughts calling for our attention. We cannot and will not hear His voice until they are quieted.

Learning to quiet your inner man can be challenging but there are steps you can take that help until it becomes a habit:
- ➢ Write down thoughts that invade with a LOUD voice.
- ➢ Focus on Jesus [**Hebrews 12:2**]
- ➢ Open the eyes of your spirit to behold what the Spirit of God wants you to 'see' and behold in a vision. **DO NOT attempt to move toward the Lord until you have stilled yourself**
- ➢ Sing spontaneous songs given by the Spirit in your heart.
- ➢ Sing the song that bubbles up in your heart until you sense release or freedom through it. By tuning into the spontaneous bubbling song within, you are learning to move by the supernatural (faint) urgings of the Spirit within.

You may find tension in your body as you become still. It could be that you're in an uncomfortable position, which is a distraction, because you are focusing on the discomfort. For instance, kneeling can bring discomfort. If you sense the need to kneel, by all means do so; however, sitting is permissible by God [**1 Chronicles 17:16**]. You can walk around or even lie down for that matter. You can enjoy the late evening or tap into the quietness of the early morning. **Do what works for you!**

Take notice of your breathing. Is it relaxed or short and fast? Take a good deep breath and breathe in the pure 'spirit of Christ' with conscious intent. Remember the goal is NOT becoming completely still. It is being still enough to sense the gentle promptings of the Holy Spirit. It cannot be forced. It must be allowed to happen.

>>**See yourself as God sees you.**<<

Don't allow the 'accuser of the brethren' [**2 Corinthians 5:21**] to bring up your past. Let's visualize ourselves clothed in the robe of righteousness. The problem is that we live our lives according to the internal vision we have on the inside of us. In other words we are *spiritual schizophrenics* because we have a conflicting picture of who we are. We are not a **saved sinner** but a saved, redeemed, and cleansed person in Christ.

Because of our distorted view we cannot move towards God because focus has shifted off of Christ and is now on us individually. Then we spend time evaluating our shortcomings [**Hebrews 12:2**].

Walking in the Supernatural Power of Prayer

Visualizing or seeing ourselves as God sees us is not a New Age practice. Other groups quiet themselves to tap into the spiritual realm for a spirit guide or to be moved by some cosmic being. This is dangerous. When we visualize, it's simply coming into alignment with how God already views us.

Once you have gotten to the point that you are still, you can begin to sense His active flow within you. His spontaneous images will begin to flow with a life of their own. His voice begins to give you wisdom and strength. You find that you are 'in the Spirit' [**Revelations 1:10**]. The more you practice becoming still, the easier it becomes and the more quickly it happens.

We are tuning to the same 'still small voice' that directed the ministry of Elijah, the great prophet of old [**1 Kings 19:11-13**]. When Elisha wanted to 'touch the divine flow', he said, "But now bring me a minstrel." And it came about when the minstrel played that the hand of the Lord came upon him [**2 Kings 3:15**]. Elisha used anointed music (dedicated and designed to worship God) to tune in to the Lord. David flowed over into intuition when he wrote the psalms, which were set to music. They were basically a record of his encounters with God. In this state of stillness Elijah and Jesus received direction and guidance for their life and ministry [**John 5:39, 40**].

Characteristics of Inner Stillness

- There is no striving. In other words you are not reaching for or wrestling for God. Don't lunge after Him. Don't force it.
- "**Let**" yourself become still.
- Live in the present tense. Don't think about what you're going to do later or what you did earlier. Living in another point in time rather than **right now** can make you become stretched, torn, and fractured.
- Open your heart and He will be there; it's grace receiving. Permit it to happen to you.
- In your stillness God takes over and you sense an active flow within you [**John 5:9, 20, 30; 8:38**]

 **Part Two: Living Out of the Voice of God**

God's original intent was intimate spirit-to-spirit fellowship. Adam walked in the 'cool of the day' with God (Jesus). Both Adam and Eve heard the voice of the Lord God. Who is 'the Lord'? It's Jesus and He has been with us since the very beginning.

It is God's desire to direct and guide our live through His voice. We are His sheep [John 10:27] and He is our Shepherd. Therefore, as sheep not only do we HEAR His voice, but we also KNOW His voice.

John 10:3-5 (NIV) The gatekeeper opens the gate for Him, and the sheep listen to His voice. He calls His own sheep by name and leads them out. When He has brought out all His own, He goes on ahead of them, and His sheep follow Him because they know His voice. But they will never follow a stranger; in fact, they will run away from him because they do not recognize a stranger's voice.

A spirit can appear in a dream, a vision, a voice, or through a medium. And it can be disguised as an angel of light, Jesus, God, a Biblical personality, a deceased family member, etc. Therefore…

Walking in the Supernatural Power of Prayer

How can we discern a spirit's identity?

♦ Demons cannot confess Jesus Christ came in the flesh.

When asked if they will confess: "Jesus Christ came in the flesh", their disguise will vanish and their demonic identity will be revealed.

1 John 4:1-3 (NKJV) Beloved, do not believe every spirit, but test the spirits, whether they are of God; because many false prophets have gone out into the world. By this you know the Spirit of God: Every spirit confesses that Jesus Christ has come in the flesh is of God, and every spirit that does not confess that Jesus Christ has come in the flesh is not of God. And this is the spirit of Antichrist, which you have heard was coming, and is now already in the world.

♦ The Holy Spirit of God cannot say: "Jesus is accursed."

God, the Holy Spirit, cannot speak of the Lord Jesus in anyway but in loving, admiring, and honoring terms. The Spirit of God will NOT speak anything negative about the person or character of Christ or His work or sacrifice.

1 Corinthians 12:3 (NKJV) Therefore I make known to you that no one speaking by the Spirit of God calls Jesus accursed, and no one can say that Jesus is Lord except by the Holy Spirit.

♦ Demon spirits <u>cannot</u> say Jesus is THEIR Lord.

Regardless of whether the evil spirit is speaking through a medium (prophet, necromancer, etc.) or directly in a vision or dream, when asked to confess Jesus is their Lord, its disguise will vanish and its evil identity will be revealed.

1 Corinthians 12:3 (NKJV) Therefore I make known to you that no one speaking by the Spirit of God calls Jesus accursed, and no one can say that Jesus is Lord except by the Holy Spirit.

These three objective tests done to discern spirits work when faithfully done

However, if the 'prophet' is lying about channeling spirits, then these tests do not apply. Humans can lie and say anything they want. Only when the spirit is speaking do these tests work.

John 17:17 (NKJV) Sanctify them by Your truth. Your word is truth.

    God does not want anything in between Him and His people. He does speak; therefore do not refuse Him who is speaking. He spoke to Israel when He delivered them from Egypt and were wandering in the wilderness. In **Deuteronomy 5:22-32** the Lord speaks to the whole assembly in a loud voice. There is no mistaking that God is speaking. And they are told to be careful to do all that the Lord has commanded.

    Then in **Hebrews 12:18-26** we are told not to refuse him who speaks. His voice shook the earth and one day He promised that his voice would not only shake the earth but also the heavens. When God speaks we cannot help but listen. Therefore, it is dangerous to determine that God only speaks in a certain way or that we can only have a relationship with God one way. This produces incorrect doctrine and a level of extreme that hinders the Gospel rather than advancing it.

Walking in the Supernatural Power of Prayer

God doesn't want a relationship with us through the Bible *only*. Paul was an excellent example of a Pharisee who had a relationship with God through the law [the Book, the Bible] only. He murdered believers because he believed he was following the commands of God correctly. It wasn't until God gave him an experience of revelation knowledge on the road to Damascus that he knew differently.

Today some Christians have built a set of rules and principles telling about God who lived and moved in miracles in days past. In fact many churches tell their congregations to not expect to hear God's voice because we now have the Bible. It's true that in the Bible we find records of people who have had a direct encounter with God through the Spirit, but what about our personal encounter or relationship with Jesus? True Christianity demands a **direct encounter** with God through Jesus Christ.

Is our relationship with God through the Bible only? Do we accept the Holy Spirit as a vital part of our walk with God?

John 14:16, 17 (NIV) And I will ask the Father, and He will give you another Advocate to help you and be with you forever – the Spirit of truth. The world cannot accept Him, because it neither sees Him nor knows Him. But you know Him, for He lives with you and will be in you.

God doesn't want a relationship with us through the Spirit only **without** the Bible. New Age followers explore the world of the spirit without the Bible to act as a compass and help them see what is right and what is wrong. Actually New Age followers want more than the false idol of *rational Christianity* (Pharisee-ism). They realize there is a spirit world and they are hungry to explore it, but the do it without the guidance of the Bible. Therefore they explore the spiritual world unprotected.

In ignorance they seek to connect with spiritual powers without discerning that there are both good and evil spiritual powers. Moreover they discover some of God and some of Satan. They have no way to discern which is which because they have discarded the Bible as the authoritative standard of truth about God and Satan.

True Christianity is where the Bible and the Holy Spirit meet. We cannot effectively walk our salvation walk without the balance of the two. In the Bible the history and documentation of God-encounters the people have had provide a track and a guideline by which we are able to gauge and measure our experiences with Almighty God.

In return, the Bible is not to replace our own experience with God. Instead it should serve as a sounding board for us, so when we have similar experience, we can compare them with those who have walked with God before us. David and Paul both prayed for and hungered for this spiritual revelation as they meditated on the Bible. Paul knew that without the spirit, he would be nothing more than a Pharisee.

Psalm 119:18 (NIV) *David* said: "Open my eyes that I may see wonderful things in your law."
Ephesians 1:17, 18 (NIV) *Paul* said: "I keep asking that the God of our Lord Jesus Christ, the glorious Father, may give you the Spirit of wisdom and revelation so that you may know Him better. I pray that the eyes of your heart may be enlightened in order that you may know the hope to which He has called you, the riches of His glorious inheritance in His holy people."

 **Part Three: Journaling – A Means of Discerning God's Voice**

Habakkuk 2:1, 2 (NIV) I will stand at my watch and station myself on the ramparts; I will look to see what he will say to me, and what answer I am to give to this complaint. Then the Lord replied: "**Write down the revelation** and make it plain on tablets so that a herald may run with it."

In our relationship with God we must endeavor to have our flesh nature stripped away and walk in the Light as He is in the light [1 John 1:5-10]. And the Holy Spirit will reveal or give us revelation knowledge. In Habakkuk we see that God commanded him to write down [journal] the revelation being given him. How does journaling actually help?

- ❖ Journaling allows us to capture God's response to us. Without journaling we will tend to analyze spontaneous flow of thought after we ask God a question, which will shift us into doubt.
- ❖ Journaling requires that we trust God and act in faith towards Him.
- ❖ Journaling allows us to stay in faith for extended periods of time and faith pleases God.
- ❖ We can test our journaling later with our spiritual covering for accuracy.

Spontaneity – the sound of God's voice, being still, vision in prayer, and ***journaling*** are keys that will unlock the treasure of God's voice within our hearts. By writing out our prayers and God's answers, we discover a great new freedom in hearing God's voice. In addition, our faith will increase when prayers are being answered. When we hear God's voice more clearly, it deepens our relationship with God through dialogue. It also deepens us personally, gives us greater balance, and precise focus. The Bible clearly illustrates in Psalms, any major or minor prophet book, and Revelation a form of journaling.

⇒**Ways in which journaling is extremely helpful in one's prayer life**⇐
- •Enables you to receive whole pages, rather than single phrases.
- •Frees you to write in faith, knowing you can test it later.
- •Keeps your mind occupied and therefore out of the way.
- •Helps you recall the message after a period of time.
- •Helps you persevere during periods of waiting.

Meditation in scripture along with journaling will open difficult and hard to understand passages.

>>Practical suggestions for journaling…
- Decide whether early morning or evening is best.
- Use a spiral bound notebook, NOT scraps of paper.
- Keep your journal in a private place. It's not for everyone's eyes.
- Mistakes are a part of journaling – master life and learn from your mistakes.
- Date all journaling, etc. Skip a line when you change from you and God speaking.
- Use symbols on sensitive areas or names.
- Journal in a time that you set aside on a regular basis. Time element depends on you and what is needed.
- Do not try to date things in your spiritual journal. Don't nail dates for specific things to happen. God's time is not our time.
- Write down the questions don't just think them.
- Re-read the last journal entry.
- After journaling for a period of weeks and months, review looking for themes and 'repeated' items.
- You should hear God's voice every time you journal. He's alive especially in YOU!
- Ask the Lord what He would like to say to you.
- Put your dreams in your journal – any figurative/symbolic language, pictures, and visions
- Tell your heart you want to remember your dreams.
- Watch out! Alarm clocks tend to shatter dream recall.

NOTES

Chapter 5
The Keys of Favor, Grace, and Mercy

There are three words which affect the life of every person. All three of these words are bestowed freely and are given from someone of a higher position like a parent with a child, or a judge to someone who is in his court room, or a rich person to a poor person, or God to man. In the gospel of [**Matthew 18:23-28**] for instance, the scripture is speaking of forgiveness. However, if a person does not find favor with someone, whether God or man, he or she will not receive forgiveness.

Favor, grace, and mercy are essential to the prayer warrior. He or she must be a person of compassion who because of the mercy of God in their life can offer favor and mercy to those they are praying for even if they are not truly worthy of it. These three powerful words are given freely. No man can earn them on their own power or ability. Yet when they are given, we can earn a deeper degree or level of them by the way we respond to them as they are bestowed on us.

Let us not be like the unfaithful servant who found favor with his king and had mercy and grace shown to him. Then immediately after leaving the king's presence, the unfaithful servant who had been forgiven a large financial debt, found another servant who owed him a small amount of money and had that servant placed in prison. When the king found out what happened he withdrew his grace and mercy from the ungrateful servant and all the favor he had received was taken from him and judgment took its place.

It seems that the willingness to forgive plays a large part in favor, grace, and mercy being shown to a person who by their own merits can never earn them. When a person who intercedes for another in prayer and applies these three words to the person who they are praying for can be assured of victory.

Biblical faith is in the realm of the heart. In [**Romans 10:10**] we find it written that 'with the heart one believes'. And hope is in the realm of the mind [**Hebrews 11:1**]. We must make the *logos* (the written word) become the ***Rhema*** (the spoken word) of God. *Logos* is the Bible on your table. ***Rhema*** is the word of God in your mouth.

Prayer is our seventh weapon. It takes the battle beyond our limit into the unlimited space of the Spirit. In prayer there are three explosive weapons: the word of God, the name of Jesus, and the blood of Jesus.

NOTES

Chapter 6
Abiding in Christ

If YOU abide in me and MY words abide in you, ask what you wish and it shall be done for you. [**John 15:7**]

- Abide means **we desire Him.**
- Abide means to be **crucified with Him.**
- Abide means to be **resurrected in Him.**
- Abide means to be **obedient to Him.**
- **Abide** means to be **in relationship with him.**

⇒**John 15:7** has a condition and a result.⇐

The condition: IF YOU abide in me
The result: than ask what you will and it shall be done.

A thought to Consider: The vine within itself does not produce life.
It is the substance which flows within the vine that produces life.

John 15:1 I am the true vine, and my Father is the husbandman.

John 15:4 Abide in me, and I in you. As the branch cannot bear fruit of itself, except it abide in the vine; no more can ye, except ye abide in me.

John 15:5 I am the vine, ye are the branches: He that abides in me, and I in him, the same brings forth much fruit: for WITHOUT me ye can do nothing.

Abiding in the true vine is like a marriage between a husband and a wife. It will bring forth fruit (birth). Jesus defined *abiding in Christ* when He likened Himself to a grapevine and believers to its branches. This picture illustrates the vital union existing between Christians and Jesus Christ.

The word, *abide*, basically means "to **remain**; to be in **unity**." Every Christian remains inseparably linked to Christ in all areas of life. We depend on Him for grace and the power to obey. We look obediently to His Word for instruction on how to live. We offer Him our deepest adoration and praise and we submit ourselves to His authority over our lives. In short, Christians gratefully know Jesus Christ is the source and sustainer of their lives.

Abiding in Christ evidences genuine salvation. The Apostle John alluded to that when he referred to teachers who defected from the truth when he said, 'they went out from us, but they were not really of us; for if they had been of us, they would have remained with us; but they went out, in order that it might be shown that they all are not of us" [**1 John 2:19**].

People with genuine faith will remain. They won't defect; they **won't deny** Christ or **abandon His truth**. Jesus reiterated the importance of abiding as a sign of real faith when He said, "If you abide in My Word, then you are truly disciples of Mine" [**John 8:31**].

[**John 6:53-71**] Jesus said to them, "Very truly I tell you, unless you eat the flesh of the Son of Man and drink His blood, you have no life in you. Whoever eats my flesh and drinks my blood has eternal life, and I will raise them up at the last day. For my flesh is real food and my blood is real drink. Whoever eats my flesh and drinks my blood remains in me, and I in them. Just as the living Father sent me and I live because of the Father, so the one who feeds on me will live because of me. This is the bread that came down from heaven. Your ancestors ate manna and died, but whoever feeds on this bread will live forever." He said this while teaching in the synagogue in Capernaum. On hearing it, many of his disciples said, "This is a hard teaching. Who can accept it?" Aware that his disciples were grumbling about this, Jesus said to them, "Does this offend you? The Spirit gives life; the flesh counts for nothing. The words I have spoken to you – they are full of the Spirit and life. Yet there are some of you who do not believe." For Jesus had known from the beginning which of them did not believe and who would betray Him. He went on to say, "This is why I told you that no one can come to me unless the Father has enabled them." From this time many of His disciples turned back and no longer followed Him. "You do not want to leave too, do you?" Jesus asked the Twelve. Simon Peter answered him, "Lord, to whom shall we go? You have the words of eternal life. We have come to believe and to know that you are the Holy One of God." Then Jesus replied, "Have I not chosen you, the Twelve? Yet one of you is a devil!"

(He meant Judas, the son of Simon Iscariot, who, though one of the Twelve, was later to betray him.)

Christ warned the disciples, "Because ye are not of the world, but I have chosen you out of the world, therefore the world hateth you" [**John 15:19**].

After giving many *positive* promises, Christ now gives a *negative* one that applies to every follower of the Lord Jesus Christ.

The governmental system of the world is opposed to Christ and therefore is opposed to those who follow Him.

Therefore the world hates Christians simply because Christ lives in them and they [the world] doesn't know God. Being the object of the world's hatred is a good indication that we are God's children.

NOTES

Chapter 7
Christ's Identity in Me

[1 Peter 2:9] But you are a chosen people, a royal priesthood, a holy nation, and God's special possession, that you may declare the praises of him who called you out of darkness into his wonderful light.

You are God's masterpiece, His tapestry.
[Ephesians 2:10]
You are one who He desires to trust in and use to bring change.

God Dwells in Us

All these things that God has done for our lives are too wonderful for us! The good news is that we do not have to rely upon ourselves to accomplish all of these great things in God for it is Christ in us that will do the work. God works in us, lives in us, speaks through us and acts through our lives. **[Matthew 10:20]**

We can say that He sees through our eyes and hears through our ears. We may be insensitive to the living presence of God in us, but if we are willing to yield ourselves completely over to the instruction of the Holy Spirit we will become aware of all that God would do in and through our members. We have been given the mind of Christ and the Spirit of the Son.

The foundation of the faith is that Christ dwells in us.**[Ephesians 3:17]** He is the greater One, Jesus, who along with the Father have made their dwelling in us by the Holy Spirit, who was given to us by the Father. He is both with us and in us. And we are to walk in Him, live in Him and conduct ourselves by His desires. We are joined to the Lord and are one Spirit with Him. We are called the temple of the Holy Ghost. We have received the same glory that the Father gave to Jesus. We are made one with Him just as He is One with the Father: Jesus is in us and the Father in Jesus so that we can be perfect in this oneness.

Walking in the New Covenant to Represent Him

One of the absolutes of the New Covenant is that we are to be those that represent God and stand in the place of Jesus. In order to fully represent Jesus, we have been given the power and authority that we need; Christ in us our confidence of glory. It was by the Holy Ghost that Jesus was incarnated into the womb of Mary and it is by the same Spirit of the Lord that we have been born again.

Jesus was baptized in the Holy Spirit to preach the gospel of the kingdom and so we too have been baptized with the same Spirit to preach this gospel of the dear Son. We are both commissioned and empowered to represent the kingdom. We are not of this world and are just like Him because we have been translated into His kingdom and baptized in His power.

Walking in the Supernatural Power of Prayer

The closer we draw to Him we discover our True Identity.

*Use these Bible verses to understand more about our identity in Christ,
and how to not lose sight of who we are destined to be.*

God created human beings to have unique characteristics and purposes. The more closely we are drawn to Him, the more we discover our true identity and the more we allow God to weave us into a beautiful tapestry of His image and His ways.

Proverbs 19:21 Many are the plans in a person's heart, but it is the Lord's purpose that prevails.

Jeremiah 29:11 (NIV) "For I know the plans I have for you," declares the LORD, "plans to prosper you and not to harm you, plans to give you hope and a future.

John 1:12 Yet to all who did receive him, to those who believed in his name, he gave the right to become children of God

Ephesians 1:5 he predestined us for adoption to son ship through Jesus Christ, in accordance with his pleasure and will

Romans 8:29-30 For those God foreknew he also predestined to be conformed to the image of his Son, that he might be the firstborn among many brothers and sisters. And those he predestined, he also called; those he called, he also justified; those he justified, he also glorified.

Colossians 2:9-10 For in Christ all the fullness of the Deity lives in bodily form, and in Christ you have been brought to fullness. He is the head over every power and authority.

1 Corinthians 6:17 But whoever is united with the Lord is one with him in spirit.

Jeremiah 1:5 Before I formed you in the womb I knew you, before you were born I set you apart; I appointed you as a prophet to the nations.

1 Corinthians 12:27 Now you are the body of Christ, and each one of you is a part of it.

Galatians 3:27-28 for all of you who were baptized into Christ have clothed yourselves with Christ. There is neither Jew nor Gentile, neither slave nor free, nor is there male and female, for you are all one in Christ Jesus.

1 Corinthians 6:19-20 Do you not know that your bodies are temples of the Holy Spirit, who is in you, whom you have received from God? You are not your own; you were bought at a price. Therefore honor God with your bodies.

1 John 3:1-2 See what great love the Father has lavished on us, that we should be called children of God! And that is what we are! The reason the world does not know us is that it did not know him. Dear friends, now we are children of God, and what we will be has not yet been made known. But we know that when Christ appears, we shall be like him, for we shall see him as he is.

Colossians 3:1-3 Since, then, you have been raised with Christ, set your hearts on things above, where Christ is, seated at the right hand of God. Set your minds on things above, not on earthly things. For you died, and your life is now hidden with Christ in God.

God Reproducing Himself In Us
By E.W. Kenyon

Every real father desires to reproduce himself in his son. The Father's dream is to reproduce Himself in us. You understand that the New Creation has received the nature and life of the Father.

We invite the Holy Spirit, who has imparted to us this Nature from the Father, to come into our body and make His home in us, then as we begin to feed on the Word, practice the Word, live the Word, He builds that Word into us.

The very genius of Christianity is the ability of God to build Himself into us through the Word, so that in our daily walk we live like the Master.

[**Ephesians 5:1,2**] "Be ye therefore imitators of God, as beloved children; and walk in love, even as Christ also loved you, and gave himself up for us." As children of Love, we are to walk in Love as Christ walked in Love toward the world. The Father so loved the world that He gave His Son. Jesus so loved the world that He gave Himself. Now I so love the world that I give myself. I don't allow my heart to grow bitter toward it, no matter what the criticism or the persecution may be.

Whenever I am inclined to say, Well, I am wasting my time on them, I remember Paul and Silas at Philippi: They had been arrested. They had been whipped until their backs were a mass of bleeding flesh, then put into a dungeon with their hands and feet in stocks. In the midst of that agony, that physical distress, they prayed and sang praises.

They so stirred Heaven that the Father had to open the jail; and when the earthquake had so frightened the jailer that he cried out in agony of fear, Paul preached to him with that bleeding back, and the jailer found Jesus. Then he washed the backs of both Paul and Silas, and a Church was formed in the home of the jailer. If Paul had any other spirit he could never have done it, but he was like his Master. He gave himself up to the dominion, the Lordship of Love.

The Father wants to reproduce Himself in us. [**Galatians 4:19**]: "My little children, of whom I am again in travail until Christ be formed in you." The process of building Christ into one may be very slow, but it makes Jesus men and women out of us.

We are created in Christ Jesus. We are His Creation; and until Christ is formed in us, the world cannot see anything but religion in us. [**Philippians 2:13**]: "For it is God who worketh in you both to will and to work, for his good pleasure." The Father is actually building His Love Life, His Righteousness, His strength, and His Wisdom into our spirits.

Years ago when I was the head of the school back in the East, after an evangelistic campaign I would invariably ask some of the teachers, "Have I grown any since you last saw me? Can you see any marks of growth in my spiritual life?" I was so fearful that a month or two would go by that I hadn't grown in Christ and in Knowledge of the Word.

[**II Peter 3:18**]: "But grow in the grace and knowledge of our Lord and Savior Jesus Christ." Grace means Love at work. The Greek word means "Love Gifts." The Spirit longs for us to grow in this Love Life; to have the Love Nature of Jesus demonstrated in our daily walk. I am convinced beyond the shadow of a doubt, that only as we yield ourselves to the Lordship of Love, can He ever build Himself into us.

It is not knowledge of the Scriptures. I may have a vast knowledge of the Word. That isn't it. It is the Word that is built into me and becomes a part of me that counts. As you study the Pauline Revelation you become convinced that the ultimate of every one of those Epistles is the building of the Jesus Life in the individual. His plan for building Himself into us is striking. We must take Jesus' place. We must learn to act in His stead. There must be the conscious training of our spirits to be His actual representatives.

[**Colossians 1:9-12**] gives us an intimation of the passion of the Father to make Himself known to us in such a real way that we can enter into all the riches of the fullness of His Life that belongs to us. Here is a prayer of the Spirit through the lips of Paul: "For this cause we also, since the day we heard it, do not cease to pray and make request for you, that ye may be filled with the knowledge of his will in all spiritual wisdom and understanding."

The word **knowledge** in the Greek is "epignosis." **It means full knowledge, complete knowledge, exact knowledge**. We should have that kind of Knowledge, for it is in this Revelation.

We have the Holy Spirit who inspired it as our teacher. He has never left His position as an instructor. He is here in my heart and yours, and He longs to fill us with the exact knowledge of the Father's will in all Spiritual Wisdom and Understanding. It will be Wisdom to use the knowledge of this Revelation in our daily walk. It will be Wisdom to know how to use the statements of fact as well as the promises in the Gospels. It will be Wisdom to know how to make this message known in an attractive way. We are to have "knowledge of His will in all spiritual wisdom," a deeper insight into the very heart of the Father.

[**I Corinthians 2:9,10**] may throw some light on this. "Things which eye saw not, the ear heard not, and which entered not into the heart of man, whatsoever things God prepared for them that love him." These are revealed to us today in this Revelation through the Spirit, for the Holy Spirit is able to search all things, yea, the deep things of God, and our recreated spirit is enabled to follow the Holy Spirit in this searching of the Riches of His Grace.

Most of these riches are in the Pauline Revelation. In [**Ephesians 3:8**] we catch a glimpse of where Paul said, "Unto me, who am less than the least of all saints, was this grace given, to preach unto the Gentiles the unsearchable riches of Christ." These unsearchable riches belong to us, but, like pearls, we have to search for them.

[**I Corinthians 2:11,12**] "For who among men knoweth the things of a man, save the spirit of the man, which is in him? even so the things of God none knoweth, save the Spirit of God." Now note carefully the next verse: "But we received, not the spirit of the world, but the Spirit which is from God; that we might know the things that were freely given to us of God. Which things also we speak, not in words which man's wisdom teacheth, but which the Spirit teacheth." We are learning to grasp this exact truth by the aid of the Spirit.

We find that in [**Colossians 1:9,10**] this knowledge of His will in all spiritual wisdom and understanding is to enable us to walk worthy of the Lord unto all pleasing. Our walk is before the world. We might say that it is a two-fold walk. One phase of it is before the Father, and the other is before the world. I am to walk worthy of the Lord before men so they will recognize this New Life in me. I am so Jesus sized (if we could coin the word), that they will become Jesus-conscious in my presence.

I knew a woman that found Christ through my ministry over the air. Her husband was a godless man and she had been a fit companion in his worldliness, but now she had found Christ. It went on for several weeks until finally one morning before he went to work, he said, "Do you know, woman, that I have been living and sleeping and eating with Jesus Christ for the last two weeks." She was a keen-minded woman, and she said, "How do you enjoy it?" Tears filled his eyes. He said, "I wish I was like that. I wish I had that something that has come into your life." You see, Jesus had so lived in her that the man could feel the presence of the Master in her.

Two young men were working in a shop. One of them was studying the Word in our classes. The fellow working on a lathe next to him said to him one morning, "Harry, I would like to ask you something that is personal. What have you in your life that makes you so different from all the other men here in the room?" The boy answered, "Jesus." "Oh," he said, "that is religion; I don't believe in that. And the young boy said, "It is not religion, it is the Living Christ."

Christ magnified in my body, said Paul [**Philippians 1:20**]; Christ made large in my daily walk. In [**Philippians 1:20,21**] he said, "For to me to live is Christ."

Once those words burned in my heart for months. The Master was saying to me, "I want to be magnified in you. I want to absorb your personality. I want to take possession of your dreams and ambitions. I want the first place in your life." I was afraid of Him. I spoke out, "Lord, I don't dare let you have control of me, for if I do I will never achieve the things for which I am so ambitious. And I shall never forget, a voice in my heart said, "I love you more than you love yourself. I am more ambitious for your success than you are. I have the ability to put you over."

I said, "Lord, don't make me preach on the streets. You will send me down into the slums. I don't want to go there Lord." I struggled again, but He was tender with me. His Wisdom became so apparent. Often in my extremities He had helped me. When I would get into difficulties He would lift me out.

Walking in the Supernatural Power of Prayer

One day I said, "Master, I will go with you. Here I am; take all of my ability. Swallow up my ambition with your own, but give me Love like your Love. Help me to so live that men can see you in me, feel you, that when I speak it will be your voice. When I lay hands on the sick it will be your hands." And then I heard a Scripture in [**Galatians 2:20**]: "I have been crucified with Christ; it is no longer I that live, but Christ liveth in me: and that life which I now live in the flesh I live in faith, the faith which is in your Master, who loved me, and gave himself up for me."

Then I said, "Now Master, I trust you and I give myself up to you." You see, when we come quietly in our heart-life to the place where we say "Yes" to Him, then He reveals Himself in us. It is not forced upon us. He doesn't drive us. He doesn't force us with sickness or the loss of property. The sickness comes because we are not aware that He can shield us.

We have gone the way of our inclinations. We have gone the way of our own desires and our plans have been worked out, reasoned out with sense knowledge. How it must hurt His heart when we are so unwise; when we do so many foolish things. When His Wisdom is at our call, His Ability awaits us, we are almost limitless. All that He is, is at our disposal, but sometimes we choose a road that leads to heartaches and disappointments.

You see, it is this forming of Christ within us. That is the secret that is the genius of the New Creation. "Wherefore, if any man is in Christ, there is a **New Creation**." It is perfect as far as it has gone, but He wants to build Himself more fully into that New Creation, and so He takes the things of Christ that are unveiled to us in the Word, and the Spirit builds them into us.

We admired the strength and courage of Jesus in His earth walk. We were thrilled at the ability that Christ manifested as He met every difficult situation. His Wisdom, gentleness and forbearance we admired, and now the Spirit wants to take all of those things that we have admired in Jesus and build them into us. Can't you see what it means? It is the Father's ambition to make us successful and to enable us to enjoy the riches that belong to us.

Walking in the Supernatural Power of Prayer

I don't know whether you have noticed it or not, but in one of the prayer Scriptures in [**John 16:23,24**], Jesus said this: "And in that day ye shall not pray to me. (This is literal). "But verily, verily, I say unto you, if ye shall ask anything of the Father, He will give it to you in my name. Hitherto have ye asked nothing in my name: ask, and ye shall receive, that your joy may be made full." Joy is something that comes into the Recreated human spirit. The natural man doesn't have it.

Hear Jesus speaking again in [**John 15:11**]: "These things have I spoken unto you, that my joy may be in you, and that your joy may be made full." That is a miracle, that Jesus' joy may be made full in me. That not only will I make Him joyful, but He imparts to me His joy. That something that makes the evangel irresistible, now fills my heart. When I speak my face will glow, my voice will be filled with the melody of heaven.

You see, when He builds himself into us and we begin to labor together with Him, we have His Life, we have His Love, yea, we have Himself. Christ then is being formed in us. Now it is no longer I but Christ.

The men who have grown deeply spiritual, are the men and women in whom the Word has had full control.

God requires of us to be Doers of the Word

[**John 15:7,8**] may throw a little light on this: "If ye abide in me, and my words abide in you." Every believer is in Christ, but His words are not in every believer. What does it mean to have His words abiding in me, gaining the absolute ascendancy, dominating me in every phase of my thinking and my life. As [Jeremiah] said, We feed upon the Word of God. Now I am feeding. I am living in that Word. I am practicing it. I am what [**James 1:22,23**] calls, "**a doer of the Word.**"

Jesus said that the doer of the Word dug deep and built his house upon the rock, and it made his house able to stand against any storm that might beat against it. He not only said that, but: He said "If ye abide in me, and my words have found their place in you, then you can ask what you will and it shall be created by the Father for you," brought into being. Oh, I see it now. I co-operate with him.

In that fifth verse he said, "I am the vine, ye are the branches." Now I can understand it. As a branch, I am going to bear His fruit. I am laboring together with Him. He and I are operating together, are identified one with the other. He is finding a place for His ability to energize and act here on the earth again.

It is like a wealthy man that finds an intelligent, young man that he can set up in business, and the young man has ability to use this wealthy man's money. Now He and I are laboring together and the Father is glorified because I am bearing much fruit, and I prove by my life my discipleship. I prove that I am growing in Grace, and I am growing in that "exact knowledge of God, in all spiritual Wisdom and Understanding, to the end that I may walk worthy of the Lord unto all pleasing." I am bearing fruit now in every good work, and I am increasing in that exact knowledge, that perfect knowledge of the Father.

You have noticed in Jesus' life that there was always a sense of sureness, a sense of certainty. There was no vacillating. He never stopped and said, "Now pray that I may have wisdom." He had it. Into our lives comes that same quiet sureness, that certainty that we know the Father's will. We are walking in it. And we are made fruitful with His ability that is at work in us. It is according to the might of His glory, and it has given to us steadfastness and long-suffering, with joy.

[**Colossians 1:12**]: "Giving thanks unto the Father, who has given us the ability to enjoy our share of the inheritance of the saints in light." This is a climax of the heart desire of the Father that we should so let Him live His Life in us, that we begin to enjoy our share of our inheritance in Christ.

We are drawing dividends on what He has done for us and in us. We are coming to enjoy the riches of His Grace.

NOTES

Chapter 8
Who I Am in God

Speak His Word out of your mouth. Sow His Word in your heart and build it into your walk.

Our hearts may fail us due to doubt, fear, unbelief, faintheartedness etc.

By proclaiming God's word OUTLOUD, it <u>will remove</u> the obstacles out of the way and be aligned with God's word which will NOT come back void. [Isaiah 55:11]

Please Note: Your brain knows your voice

- ➤ I am born of God [**1 John 5:1**]. I am OF God [**1John 4:6**]. I am a spirit being – born of God!

- ➤ I am a spirit. I have a soul, and I live in a body, but I am first a spirit being – BORN OF GOD. [**1 Thessalonians 5:23**]

- ➤ I am a new creature in Christ, old things have passed away, behold all things have become new. [**2 Corinthians 5:17**]

- ➤ I have a new nature. It's the nature of God. It's the nature of love, for love is of God. [**1 John 4:7**]

- ➤ I have a nature of faith, because faith works by love, and the love of God has be SHED ABROAD in my heart by the Holy Ghost, who has been given to me. [**Romans 5:5**]

- ➤ I have been given the privilege of becoming a child of God. I am God's very own child and God is my very own Father. [**John 1:12; Romans 8:15**]

- ➤ Because I am His child, I am an heir of God and a joint heir with Jesus Christ. [**Romans 8:17**]

- ➤ Because I am in Christ Jesus – right now – there is no spirit of condemnation in me. [**Romans 8:1**]

- ➤ I have faith in God. I believe in Him, and I am in Him. I believe He is able and faithful.

- ➤ I am justified by FAITH; therefore, I have peace with God. [**Romans 5:17**]

- ➤ I am in Christ and He has made unto me wisdom, righteousness, sanctification, and redemption. Therefore, I am righteous in Christ Jesus and I have His wisdom. I am sanctified and redeemed by His blood. [**1 Corinthians 1:30**]

- ➤ I have the wisdom of God. I fear Him and His wisdom has been given to me.

- I have received an abundance of grace and the gift of righteousness and I reign in this life through Jesus Christ. [**Romans 5:17**] I receive and reign through Jesus Christ.

- I have been delivered from the power and the dominion of darkness (Satan) and I have been translated into the kingdom of God's dear Son. [**Colossians 1:13**]

- I have been crucified with Christ and I have been raised up together with Him and made to sit down together in heavenly places in Christ Jesus, far above all principalities, powers, might, and dominion. [**Ephesians 2:5, 6; 1:21**]

- I am presented to God as holy, without blame and reproof in His sight. Right now He freely accepts me through His grace. [**Colossians 1:22; Ephesians 1:6; 2:8**]

- I am blessed with all spiritual blessings in heavenly places in Christ, and I stand holy and without blame before Him in love. [**Ephesians 1:3, 4**]

NOTES

Chapter 9
The Holy Spirit vs. The Spirit of Christ

Question: Who is the Holy Spirit? **Answer:** He is as much God as the Father is.

For there are three who bear record in Heaven: the Father, the Word and the Holy Ghost and these are the three in one. [**I John 5**]

In **Genesis 1** we see the Holy Spirit moving on the face of the earth to prepare it for the restoration. It was by the power of the Holy Spirit that the Father raised Christ from the dead.

In every man who is born again, we have three spirits in us.

The first is the *reborn spirit*, which must feed on the word daily to grow strong. If we don't draw near to God and rebuke the devil and resist the social life of the world then we can lose our relationship with God. God sent us a Helper to teach us what we should do. Remember Jesus' word before he ascended on high, "behold I send the promise of my Father upon you, But tarry ye in the city of Jerusalem until ye be endowed from power from on high." [**Luke 24:49**] We know we are to seek the Holy Spirit and allow Him to fill us completely.

Here are some of things he does.

- He brings all things all things to remembrance.
- He gives gifts to men.
- He reveals truth to us.
- He gives us the ability to accept and confess Christ as Lord.
- He creates a new mind in us.
- He transforms us into the image of the second Adam.

The Holy Spirit is very gentle and can be grieved.

He can give us understanding. It seems that the Holy Spirit is the person of the trinity who sends messengers to man, like He did to Gabriel and who He sent to Daniel, the mother of Sampson, Elizabeth, and Mary.

Remember the Holy Spirit will come to you and fill you completely.

What does the Spirit of Christ do for us?
It gives us the authority to overcome the enemy of your soul like Jesus had.

The spirit of Christ gives you the ability to stand. "It is NO longer I that lives but Christ that lives in me. I live this life by Christ who strengthens me." [**Galatians 2:20**]

The spirit of Christ that is within us gives us the **strength to stand** against the enemy and his allies.

The Holy Spirit renews our mind daily through the word of God so we can obtain wisdom, understanding, and knowledge

The Heavens

3rd Heaven: The Throne of God

- **The Four Living Creatures** *Ezekiel 1:5*
- **Wheel**
- **Cherubims Seraphims Arch Angels**
- **Redeemed Mankind**

2nd Heaven: The Throne of Satan

- **Principalities**
- **Powers of this world**
- **Rulers of Darkness**
- **Wicked Spirits in high places**

1st Heaven: The Air Around Us

- **Wind**
- **Rain Snow**
- **Clouds**
- **Storms**
- **The air we breathe**

The Earth

- **Mankind**
- **Animals Birds**
- **Creatures of he waterways**
- **Demons**

Hell

- **The place of the Lost**
- **The holding place until the final judgement**

Chapter 10
Praying From the Third Heaven

Ephesians 2:6 (KJV) And hath raised us up together, and made us sit together in heavenly places in Christ Jesus:

>>We are seated in heavenly places!<<

It is in **Ephesians 2** that we find we are not earthbound. In other words, we are not restricted to or limited to the earth or material existence. Since that is the case then, we are **NOT** beneath the feet of our adversary and his allies where we are doomed to be defeated by him and taken captive at any time he so desires to do so.

Clearly we are not on the same level of the enemy where he can still overcome us, and enslave us at his will. If we are *below* him or even at the *same level* he is, then he can hinder our prayer before they get to the throne of God. Likewise, they can also hinder the answers to our prayers and keep them from being manifested.

In the book of Daniel, we read that Daniel prayed and fasted for twenty-one days before he received his answer. Gabriel, who was given the mission to bring Daniel the answer, was hindered from doing so by the principality over the Medes and Persians. This strongman of the kingdom of Satan was able to hold Gabriel at bay for twenty-one days [**Daniel 11**].

It wasn't until Michael, the defender of Israel, came to his aid that Gabriel was able to slip away and bring to Daniel the answer to his prayer. In fact, Gabriel told Daniel that on the very first day his prayers were received that the answer was sent to him. However, when Gabriel got to the second heaven, the power prince of the Medes and Persians rose up to hinder him.

Certainly it is good that we pray here on earth; nevertheless, it is imperative to remember that being here, we are under the feet of the Adversary. His throne is in the second heaven. Christ's first coming changed all of this for mankind. Essentially, He made a way for us to be seated with Him in the third heaven. Now this is far above any principality or power, or wicked spirit.

How is this possible? It is only because Christ has *invited* us to be seated with Him in the third heaven. Granted, our physical bodies may be stuck here on earth but our spirits are sitting with Christ far above our enemies.

We are able to speak with our Lord face to face to make our petitions known and to receive our answer directly from Him. How do we get there from here? We do this simply by letting the Spirit of God bring us there.

Walking in the Supernatural Power of Prayer

    I understand it can hard to fully comprehend this truth. Regardless of whether we grasp it or not the truth is that if we are true believers, then God has made a way for us to be there with our Lord.

    The reality is this: if we are seated with Christ far above all rulers, principalities, powers, and wicked spirits, then they are ***under our feet*** and ***have no power over us***. It's God's word! And God **cannot** lie.

We are **NOT** like the earthbound eagle covered with pestilence and can no longer fly free. No!

We are the like eagles who have shaken the pestilence off and once more stretch their wings and fly high in the heavens where nothing can touch them. We rule with the Lord by His grace and Satan doesn't rule over us.

Hearken to the saying my wife loves to repeat:

FLY EAGLE, FLY!
Isaiah 40:31

NOTES

Walking in the Supernatural Power of Prayer

Heaven Waits on YOU for Earth to Move

He is DESPERATE for US!   Are We DESPERATE for HIM?

The article by Watchman Nee, below looks at how God, in His sovereignty, chose to make His people co-laborers with Him. One of the ways that is manifested is that many times He chooses to give birth to His purposes through the prayers of His people.

This is why past revivals were historically preceded by united prayer

Such perspective underscores the enormous opportunity and privilege that we have, in coming together in one heart and one mind, in one accord, at our united multi-church monthly prayer meetings. It also underscores the perils of giving room to division, and of neglecting the pursuit of unity and united corporate prayer. To the extent we are united or divided, we either have or lack the spiritual authority that God would give us

In **[Matthew 18:18-20],** Jesus reveals that a powerful and profound thing happens when even a very small number of people in the church are united in prayer.

Five Foundational Truths that Serve as the Basis for Corporate Prayer

1. Heaven Waits for Earth to Move

"There must be a move on earth before there is a move in heaven. It is not heaven that binds first but the earth. It is not heaven that looses first but the earth."
Ref: Watchmen Nee, "The Prayer Ministry of the Church,"

Scripture reveals that God waits on His people to pray before He will act!

* **Ezekiel 22:30, Jeremiah 33:3, Psalm 107**

Jesus told his disciples "Ask, Seek, and Knock" and heaven would answer!

"Man has been given power to make way for, or to obstruct the power of God."
Ref: Watchman Nee, "Gathered In His Name," p. 141

* **Isaiah 59:1, 2 (The Message)**

In Nazareth, Jesus' power was restricted and limited by unbelief.

"How greatly restricted is heaven by earth!"
Ref: Watchman Nee, "Gathered In His Name," p. 15

When Heaven is silent and God is not moving mightily it always comes down to a failure on the earth and in the church to pray!

Walking in the Supernatural Power of Prayer

* Isa. 64:7- "No one calls on your name or strives to lay hold of you."

Elijah had to build the altar and pray first before there was fire and rain from heaven!

"The aim of the prayer meeting is to get heaven open and the glory down."

2. The Meaning and Significance of "Binding" and "Loosing"

The words binding(deo) and loosing(luo) are in the perfect tense in the original giving them a very significant meaning. **[Rev. 20:2; Rev. 5:2; I John 3:8]**

"Truly I tell you, whatever you forbid and declare to be improper and unlawful on earth must be what is already forbidden in heaven, and whatever you permit and declare proper and lawful on earth must be what is already permitted in heaven."
[Matthew 18:18] (Amplified Bible)

The ministry of the church is to pray that everything contrary to God's will in heaven is bound on earth and everything in harmony with His will is released in the earth!

"True prayer begins at the heart of God, is made known to the hearts of men, is
prayed back to God again, and God answers. This is more than a definition; it is, I
believe, the principle of God's working in the universe."
Ref: Watchman Nee, "Gathered In His Name," p. 140

Prayer originates in God's heart and is revealed to the Church through the Holy Spirit: **[Romans 8:26-27]** and **[Colossians 1:9]**.

Jesus taught his disciples to pray simply, "your kingdom come, your will be done on earth as it is in heaven." **[Matt. 6:10]**

"God shows what He wants, we stand and ask, and God acts from heaven: this is true
prayer, and this is what we must see fully expressed in our prayer meetings."
Ref: Watchman Nee, "Gathered In His Name," p. 143

When the church prays together the real focus should be on what is in God's heart—that, His Kingdom, His Power, and His Glory be released and revealed on earth as it is in heaven!

"Real prayer, truly, is full of intense desire, but it just as
intensely seeks to know the divine will."

"This is the confidence we have in approaching God: that if we ask anything according to his will, he hears us. And if we know that he hears us—whatever we ask—we know that we have what we asked of him." ~**[1 John 5:14-15]**

Walking in the Supernatural Power of Prayer

3. A Praying Church is Heaven's Outlet of Power on the Earth

"She (the church) is to be heaven's outlet, the channel of release for heaven's power, the medium of accomplishment of God's purpose. Many things have accumulated in heaven because God has not yet found His outlet on earth; the Church has not yet prayed."
Ref: Watchman Nee, "Gathered In His Name," p. 143

* [**Acts 1:8**] Jesus said: "You (the church) will receive power…"

* According to Jesus, two believers united in prayer is a powerful force on the earth!

= **The Bible speaks of the power of 2 or 3 to accomplish God's will.**=

* Aaron and Hur kept Moses' hands up and won the battle [**Exodus 17:9-16**]

* Two are better than one [**Ecclesiastes 4:9-12**]

* Jesus sent his disciples out two by two and gave them power and authority [**Luke 9 and 10**]

* Paul and Silas chained together in a prison cell experienced the power of two praying in agreement [**Acts 16**]

+ **Sadly, the most common reason for why pastors and churches stop having prayer meetings is because of small numbers in attendance!**

God likes to display His great power through small numbers of people, just ask Gideon:
"But the Lord said to Gideon, 'There are still too many men…" [**Judges 7:4**]

"The church is to secure for God the release of His power into the world…-
I speak reverently -"
Ref: Watchman Nee, "Gathered In His Name," p. 142

"Now to him who is able to do immeasurably more than all we ask or imagine, according to his power that is at work within us, to him be glory in the church…"
[**Ephesians 3:20**]

4. Unity Precedes Prayer

* The context of Jesus' words in [**Matthew 18:18-19**] is church unity.

* Jesus' teaching about praying for God's kingdom to come is quickly followed by the focus on forgiving those who have sinned against us.

* Nearly everywhere that prayer is mentioned in the New Testament the need for love, unity, and forgiveness is near by.

Walking in the Supernatural Power of Prayer

The Greek word for agree is symphonesis (meaning to be in harmony or agreement) from the root phone(o), to make sound, speak, voice.

* [**Matthew 18:19**] (Amplified)

+ **The unity and agreement among believers is the key to God's kingdom, power and glory being released in the church.**

=We see the emphasis on unity throughout the Word:=

* [**Romans 15:5-7, 1 Timothy 2:8, 1 Corinthians 1:10, Philippians 4:2**] +

If members of the body are not in unity (practicing love, acceptance, forgiveness) they will never agree in prayer and without prayer they will never fully experience the outpouring of the Holy Spirit!

[Acts 2] speaks of a corporate outpouring of the Holy Spirit because of corporate unity about waiting on God in prayer. God wants to do this again!

Ref: Speaking of Pentecost and the Spirit, A. W. Tozer said:

"He did not come to bring them into oneness of accord; He came because they were already so. The Spirit never comes to give unity (though His presence certainly aids and perfects such unity as may exist). He comes to that company who have, through repentance and faith, brought their hearts into one accord."
Ref: A.W. Tozer, "The Paths of Power,"

*[**Acts 4:24, 31**]

* Jesus expressed His will in [**John 17**]- "May they be brought to compete unity to let the world know that you sent me…"

*[**Joshua 6**] is a model of what God desires to do in and through the Church- "when the people gave a loud shout, the wall collapsed…" [**Joshua 6:20**]

"Nothing more surely marks the sad condition of churches throughout the world than the absence of the Christian Amen."

Chapter 11
My Consecration as a Christian
(Reprinted from: Adventures in God – by: John G. Lake)

I, this day, consecrate my entire life to glorify my Heavenly Father by my obedience to the principles of Jesus Christ through the power of the Holy Spirit. All my effort from now on will be directed in an effort to demonstrate the righteousness of God in whatsoever I may be engaged.

♦ Principle 1 ♦

All the earthly things that I possess shall not be considered my own, but belonging to my Heavenly Father, and shall be held in trust by me to be used and directed by the wisdom of the Spirit of God, as the law of love of men as Christ loved them may dictate.

If at any time God should raise up men wiser than myself, I will gladly commit my all to their use and turn over all my possessions to them for distribution.

If at any time in my life I should be engaged in any earthly business and should employ men to aid me in conducting it, I shall reward them justly and equally, comparing their own energy expended with my own after adding a sufficient amount to my own to cover all risk that may be involved in the operation of my business.

I shall consider my employees my equals with rights to the blessings of nature and life equal to my own. I shall not strive to elevate myself to a position of comfort above the rest of my employees and shall direct all my efforts to bring all mankind to an equal plane, where all enjoy the comforts of life and fellowship together.

♦ Principle 2 ♦

I shall not cease to cry to God and implore Him to deliver mankind from the effects of sin so long as sin lasts, but shall cooperate with God in the redemption of mankind.

I will have seasons of prayer and fasting on behalf of mankind, weeping and bewailing their lost condition and imploring God to grant them repentance unto life as the Spirit of God may lead me.

♦ Principle 3 ♦

I shall live my life in meekness, never defending my own personal rights, but shall leave all judgment to God Who judges righteously and rewards all according to their works.

I shall not render evil for evil or railing for railing, but shall bless all and do good to enemies in return for evil.

By God's grace I shall keep all hardness and harshness out of my life and actions, but shall be gentle and unassuming, not professing above what God has imparted to me, nor lifting myself above my brethren.

♦ Principle 4 ♦

I shall consider righteous acts as more necessary to life and happiness than food and drink, and not let myself be bribed or coerced into any unrighteous action for any earthly consideration.

♦ Principle 5 ♦

By God's grace I will always be merciful, forgiving those who have transgressed against me and endeavoring to correct the ills of humanity instead of merely punishing them for their sins.

♦ Principle 6 ♦

I shall not harbor any impure thoughts in my mind, but shall endeavor to make my every act uplifting.

I shall regard my procreative organs sacred and holy and never use them for any purpose other than that which God created them for.

I shall regard the home as sacred and shall always guard my actions in the presence of the opposite sex, so as not to cause a man and his wife to break their vows to one another. I shall be chaste with the opposite sex who is married, considering them as sisters (brothers). I shall be careful not to cause them undue pain by playing on their affections.

♦ Principle 7 ♦

I will always strive to be a peacemaker. First, by being peaceful myself and avoiding all unfruitful contentions, and treating all with justice and regarding their rights and their free agency, never trying to force any to my point of view.

If I should offend anyone knowingly, I shall immediately apologize.

I will not scatter evil reports about any person and so try to defame their character, or repeat things that I am not certain of being true.

I will strive to remove the curse of strife among brethren by acting as a peacemaker.

♦ Principle 8 ♦

I shall not become discouraged when I am persecuted on account of the righteousness mentioned above nor murmur on account of any suffering I undergo, but shall gladly give my life rather than depart from this high standard of life, rejoicing because I know I have a great reward in Heaven.

I shall strive to make the above principles the ideal of all the world and give my life and energy to see mankind get their power from God to practice the same.

NOTES

Chapter 12
What Obedience Produces

Obedience will bring forth the fulfillment of God's plans in your life and bring forth answers to prayer.

Obedience **IS**:

- ➢ The voluntary lifestyle of the believer, observing with the intention to keep and to do all God has commanded.
- ➢ To retire or withdraw from one's own desires; to be teachable and pliable [**Galatians 6:3**]
- ➢ Action with attitude. It comes from the heart.
- ➢ Without submission – slavery.
- ➢ The answer to a good and pure conscience [**1 Timothy 3:9; 2 Timothy 1:3; Hebrews 13:18; 1 Peter 3:16**]

Obedience **IS NOT**:

- ➢ A simple request to the believer. It is a command.
- ➢ A display of rituals, formalities and offerings [**Galatians 4:9, 10**]
- ➢ Something we do because of a reward.
- ➢ Something we do to avoid a guilty conscience.

King Saul is the perfect example of what obedience is not [**1 Samuel 10:8; 13:1-10; 15:3-23**]. Saul's problem was that he adhered to rituals, ceremonies, and sacrifices. However, God desires obedience above sacrifices. He delights in the person who follows the instruction He commands. And God requires complete obedience, not partial. In fact, there is no such thing as partial obedience.

There are results of obedience and loving obedience. [**Psalms 119:97-105, 129-136, 165-174**] The love of obedience will cause us to meditate on the word of God and by doing this we keep it [**Joshua 1:8**]. It will also keep us from sin [**Psalm 119:9, 101-104**], give us direction and guidance [**Psalm 119:105**], and ultimately will give us great peace [**Psalm 119:165**].

Obedience was the one virtue or the one requirement of the Garden of Eden (Paradise) [**Genesis 2:16, 17; 3:11**]. In fact Paradise, Calvary, and Heaven all proclaim in one voice, "Obedience is the first and the last thing your God requires of you." [**Romans 5:19; Philippians 2:8, 9; Hebrews 5:8, 9; Revelation 22:14**]

Men of Obedience

Old Testament	New Testament
Noah [**Genesis 6:22; 7:5**]	Jesus Christ [**John 10:18; Romans 5:19; Hebrews 10:9**]
Abraham [**Genesis 22:16-18; Hebrews 11:7**]	Peter [**Acts 5:32; 1 Peter 1:2, 14, 15, 22**]
Moses [**Exodus 19:5**]	Paul [**Romans 1:5; 16:26**]

In Jesus Christ obedience:
- Was a life principle [**John 6:38**]
- Was a joy [**Psalm 40:8; John 4:34**]
- Led to waiting of God's will [**Psalm 40:6-8**]
- Was unto death [**John 6:38**]
- Sprang from the deepest humility [**Philippians 2:5-8**]
- Was of faith, in entire dependence upon God's strength [**John 5:30**]

James 1:22 (KJV) Be ye doers of the word, and not hearers only, deceiving your own selves.
1 John 2:3, 4 (KJV) And hereby we do know that we know Him, if we keep His commandments. He that saith, I know Him, and keepeth not His commandments, is a liar, and the truth is not in him.
1 John 3:18-22 (KJV) My little children, let us not love in word, neither in tongue; but in deed and in truth. And hereby we know that we are of the truth, and shall assure our hearts before Him. For if our heart condemn us, God is greater than our heart, and knoweth all things. Beloved, if our heart condemn us not, then have we confidence toward God. And whatsoever we ask, we receive of Him, because we keep His commandments, and do those things that are pleasing in His sight.
1 John 5:3 (KJV) For this is the love of God, that we keep His commandments: and His commandments are not grievous.

Disobedience will withhold God's blessings from you like love and forgiveness [**Matthew 5:44; Mark 11:25; John 13:34**]. Disobedience will not allow the word to grow in your life and prayers are left unanswered [**Joshua 1:8; John 15:7**]. You witness by telling others of the good news of Jesus Christ is hindered [**Mark 16:15**]. Your church attendance will wane and fellowship with fellow believers will be broken [**Hebrews 10:25**]. Thanksgiving and praise will not flow from your lips. Worry, murmuring, anger, and discouragement is not thanksgiving and praise [**Philippians 4:6; 2:14**].

Faith works by love [**Galatians 5:6**]. <u>Love cannot work without obedience</u>. When you love God and you are in complete obedience to His word, there is absolutely nothing that can stand in your way and hinder your faith. Cain and Abel are excellent examples between obedience and disobedience [**Genesis 4:1-7**]

What is the secret of true obedience [**Hebrews 5:8, 9**]? Because of our sinful nature, obedience is not something we inherently and easily desire to do. Obedience is learned and our teacher and greatest example is Christ, Himself [**John 12:49, 50**]. Our textbook is the Bible [**Matthew 4:4, 7, 10; Luke 24:27**]. Jesus was a man of the word, but the word without the Spirit has no power to work obedience. Since Christ is the teacher, then we are the students. We must give our wholehearted attention to the teacher. When we learn obedience, it will bring forth the fulfillment of God's plan for our lives.

NOTES

Chapter 13
The Authority Abiding in Us

Everyone wants to walk in power and authority by healing the sick, casting out devils, doing the works of Jesus, dominating the circumstances of life, and ruling and reigning with Christ in the here and now. There is only one way in which this can happen. WE HAVE TO DIE! The new birth (being saved) is death to the old man [**Romans 6:1-19; 2 Corinthians 5:17; Colossians 3:3**]

In other words we are now dead to sin and alive to God. He has raised us up together and made us sit together in heavenly places in Christ [**Ephesians 2:6**]. So…does hell know who we are? If they do, do we know who we are?

Dead Men Walking

1 Peter 4:1, 2	When Christ died…	We died.
Galatians 2:20	When Christ was raised from the dead…	We were raised from the dead.
1 Peter 3:18, 19	When Christ went to Hell and suffered…	We went to Hell and suffered.

Christ died a substitutionary death. He took our place. Because of this we can identify with Christ because WE ARE IN HIM!

The reason the wicked one cannot touch us is because he can't find us. Our lives are hidden with Christ in God [**Psalm 91, Proverbs 18:10**]. If we desire to exercise God's authority here on the earth as Jesus did, then we must lay down our lower life and take up His higher life. [**1 Corinthians 9:24-27; 1 Peter 2:21-24**]

To have authority means to have power, to take charge or to take dominion. From the very beginning God who has ALL authority gave man dominion and authority [**Genesis 1:26-28; Psalm 8:4-8**]. However Adam allowed Satan to deceive him in the Garden. As a result of Adam's sin, man failed to walk in authority and lost the image of Christ.

Great news! Jesus regained man's authority by dying on a cross and getting the keys to the kingdom [**Matthew 16:19; 18:18, 19**]. He exercised this kind of authority here on earth and showed us how to operate in this authority [**Luke 8:22-25; Hebrews 2:16, 17; Philippians 2:5-8**]. Now we can unlock heaven's treasures and those who are bound. We can also lock out Satan's activities in our lives. Our authority has to be exercised [**Matthew 28:18-20**]. And the only thing keeping us from having authority is allowing Satan to deceive us.

Six areas we have authority over are:
- Sin [**Romans 6:14**]
- Sickness [**1 Peter 2:24**]
- Thought life [**2 Corinthians 10:5**]
- Fear [**2 Timothy 1:7**]
- Confusion [**1 Corinthians 14:33**]
- The enemy [**Luke 10:19**]

Walking in the Supernatural Power of Prayer

Authority begins with submission

To be effectual, we need to be submitted to God's word and His will [**James 4:7, 10**]. In **Luke 7:2-9**] the Roman centurion understood how authority operated. God who has ALL authority delegated authority to us. When we speak with His authority, we speak for Him. Who should we be submitted to?
- ♦ We should be submitted to one another [**Ephesians 5:21**].
- ♦ We should be submitted to those in authority over us [**Hebrews 13:7**].
- ♦ When children, we should be submitted to our parents [**Ephesians 6:1**].
- ♦ We should be submitted to human institutions and authority [**1 Peter 2:13**].
- ♦ We should be submitted to elders [**1 Peter 5:5**].
- ♦ We should not be conformed to this world [**Romans 12:1, 2**]
- ♦ Wives should be submitted to husbands [**Ephesians 5:22**].
- ♦ We should buffet ourselves [**1 Corinthians 9:27**].

Great authority can only be given to those who have an understanding of submission and a servant's heart. Jesus, the Word, knew servant hood and gave us the example by taking on the form of a bondservant [**Philippians 2:7; Luke 22:24-27; John 13:4-17; Matthew 20:25-28**]. In the Greek the right to act is *exousia* and the ability or the power is *dunamis*. We are to be strong in this delegated authority given to us by the Word.

When Satan sees us using our authority, he must flee [**James 4:7**]. We exercise this authority by using Jesus' name [**Philippians 2:9**], the Word of God [**Luke 4:32; Matthew 8:5, 8; John 15:7; Ephesians 6:17; Hebrews 4:12**], and His blood [**Matthew 26:28; 1 Peter 1:19; Hebrews 10:19; Psalm 91:5-7**]. The devil is scared of the authority given to us and that is why he will try to keep us from learning the truth about our authority in Christ. When we discover our authority as believers, Satan is defeated and overcome.

Imagine if every believer understood their authority and stood together in unity! There is a spiritual power in unity that we need to understand. At the Tower of Babel [**Genesis 11: 1-9**], the people tapped into the power of unity. However, they were operating under their own will and not in submission to the Lord so this power could have been very destructive. This is why God intervened and shattered their ability to come into one voice.

Amazing! If people not submitted to God could wield such power, what would happen if there were those submitted to God? I am speaking of the power of unity that is available to the church that walks as Jesus spoke about in [**John 17**] – in a oneness that mirrors that of the Father and the Son.

[**Acts 2:1-6**] shows God's divine redemption and restoration of the true unity that had been defiled by human will at Babel. One hundred twenty believers were gathered in the upper room to wait upon Him. Unlike the people at the Tower of Babel, they were not trying by their own strength to reach their own goals. They were simply submitted to the Lord and waiting for the promise of the Holy Spirit.

As they did, they experienced a supernatural visitation where the Holy Spirit filled them. As they spoke only what the Spirit gave them to speak, the Lord supernaturally enabled all the people around them to hear the same message – God being praised – each in their own language. For the first time since Babel, the power of true unity was realized and the result was a harvest of three thousand souls and an explosion of the church in a single day.

Walking in the Supernatural Power of Prayer

In many ways the church is still functioning in an Old Testament model when it comes to authority. In the Old Testament, God would anoint an individual – a prophet, a priest, or a king – who would be given the authority by the Lord to lead. However in Acts we see the Spirit of God rested not on just one man but on a corporate body of one hundred twenty.

As we move more into a model of the kingdom, we should expect to see a body of believers, carrying the same spirit, passion and heart that will rise in unity to walk together. It is my personal belief that the early church walked in a revelation of this corporate anointing.

Over time as religious rules replaced relationship with God and one another, the church entered a period where many truths the Lord had poured in at its inception were lost, including the principle of corporate unity that releases authority.

Although the church has the potential to exercise an authority to address powers and principalities at city, region, or nation-wide levels, we have not yet seen this authority demonstrated. This is because no one individual, ministry, or denomination no matter how anointed they are, or how much revelation they have, can exercise this level of authority alone. It is a corporate authority that is required that can only be released through true unity.

The key to corporate unity is corporate death, humility, and brokenness that bring us into a place of submission to the Lord and to one another. We need to come to the place of being willing to die even to the gifts and visions the Lord has given us. It's **not** about laying down our giftings and **not** using them, but it's about **dying** to our **right** to use them to build our own vision or ministry. It's not about canceling what we do but it's about allowing the Holy Spirit to channel it for the corporate when and how He sees fit.

If a remnant of believers will humble themselves to walk in true unity they can operate in a spiritual authority far more powerful than any amassing of human strengths. By 'laying down our crowns' at the feet of the Lord Jesus, we submit ourselves as a corporate body to seek the Lord together, refusing to move until He speaks. And once we have heard Him and come into agreement of a clear witness (it seems right to us and the Holy Spirit) as to His direction and timings, then will we begin to move with the authority of heaven and to address principalities and powers over our cities, regions, and nations.

>> Praying in Jesus Name <<

All Authority that was given to Jesus IS given to US
Matthew 28:18

Matthew 28:18 (KJV) And Jesus came and spake unto them, saying, All power is given unto me in heaven and in earth.

God the Father gave all authority to Jesus and then He sat down on His throne. Like wise Jesus gave the Church (us) all power and authority [**Ephesians 1:19-21**] and He sat down at the right hand of God. Now we have the authority on earth through the name of Jesus. The more we understand this authority the stronger our faith becomes and the more effective our weapon becomes.

John 14:12-14 (KJV) Verily, verily, I say unto you, He that believeth on me, the works that I do shall he do also; and greater works than these shall he do; because I go unto my Father. And whatsoever ye shall ask in my name, that will I do, that the Father may be glorified in the Son. If ye shall ask any thing in my name, I will do it.

His name carries the authority because authority was given to Him. And we've been given His name and pray *in Jesus' name* because His name is above every name. We do not pray to Jesus but we pray to the Father in Jesus' name [**John 16:23**]. Essentially we are to walk by the Spirit and when the Spirit leads us, we can speak with the same authority Jesus did.

Satan and his demon spirits know whether or not we have the authority and power over them and they react accordingly. They either flee at our command or they will ignore us. The seven sons of Sceva did not have the authority to cast out demons [**Acts 19:13-15**]. We are given authority to the degree we are under authority. Basically, the more we submit to the Lordship of Jesus, the more power and authority we have. When we do this and use His name in prayer, this is the authority Satan bows to.

>>Rebelling against God's authority<<

Satan was cast out of heaven because he rebelled against God's authority. We too can rebel against God's authority by going our own way instead of doing His will. When this happens we are not under authority; therefore, we have no authority. Jesus had authority because He did the will of the Father. The seven sons of Sceva used the name of Jesus but they had no power or authority because they were not under the Lordship of Jesus.

>>Faith works where God directs it<<

Jesus did what the Father showed Him to do. In [**Acts 10:38**] we find Peter is at Caesarea and he is talking to Cornelius and his household. He is telling them that Jesus was anointed with the Holy Spirit and then healed all who were oppressed by the devil. And we have this same anointing when we speak the will of God in Jesus' name, God will make it happen,

Walking in the Supernatural Power of Prayer

Why Didn't the Lame Man Walk?

The lame man in [**Acts 3:1-8**] had been at the temple when Jesus was still here on earth. In fact Jesus walked by him every day when He went into the temple; however, Jesus never healed him. Why not? Jesus didn't heal him because the Holy Spirit never directed Him to do so.

When the words written in the Bible become real to us and we know inside without a doubt the words are true, God makes things happen.[**Hebrews 11**] is full of the accounts of people who believed the word in this way.

By reading the word, we determine the will of God.

By prayer, the written word becomes real to us.

Please Note: Doing this we will walk in **His authority** to accomplish God's will on the earth, and our joy will full when our prayers are answered.

NOTES

Chapter 14
Prayer Warfare is Spiritual Warfare
The Bigger Picture

When we speak of spiritual warfare we are essentially speaking of the conflict between God and His heavenly host and Satan and his evil forces. To engage in this spiritual warfare is through prayer. Spiritual warfare is prayer warfare. We can only fight from two basic strategies: defensive or offensive. Consider this – those who fight offensively takes the initiative. Napoleon Bonaparte was asked, "How did you win all your battles?" His reply was, "I was always there a few minutes before they expected me."

We must discern the nature of Satan's lie. For instance you may have thoughts like: he will never get saved, he will never change, you will never get healed, or you will never have enough. We can exercise our authority in Jesus to stop Satan's activities. God's word says:

⇒ Take every lie into captivity of the word – **2 Corinthians 10:5**
⇒ Bind the strongman – **Mark 3:27**
⇒ Plunder his goods – **Mark 3:27**
⇒ Bind his rule and authority – **1 Corinthians 15:24**

Prayer can alter history by releasing legions of angels into action. Realizing this should motivate us to pray intently and constantly. **2 Chronicles 7:14** says, If my people, which are called by my name, shall humble themselves, and pray, and seek my face, and turn from their wicked ways; then will I hear from heaven, and will forgive their sin, and will heal their land.

⇒ **What happens in the heavenlies when we engage in spiritual warfare?**

Unseen to the natural eye, angels engage in battle in the spiritual world. Individually or collectively as we pray, they may guide the governments of the earth as well as events in our own personal lives.

We can see a glimpse into the continual battle raging in the spiritual realm between those angels protecting God's people and those angels trying to destroy God's people in **Daniel 10**. Daniel was praying for direction and clarification. After **twenty-one days**, angel came and told him God had heard his prayer the **very first day** and had dispatched the angel to him (Daniel) with the answer [**Daniel 10:12, 13, 20, 21**].

Contemplate the contrast between the natural and spiritual. A spiritual battle is happening in an effort to control the movement of the nations. In history (natural) several battles took place between Persia and Greece.

<u>Ephesians 6:10-12</u> We do not wrestle with flesh and blood but with unseen spiritual forces.

We play a major part in the unseen battle by praying. Daniel prayed twenty-one days. He set his heart on understanding [**Daniel 10:12**]. Just like Daniel we need to be persistent and determined. We need to put on our armor [**Ephesians 6**] and pray the word cause angels hearken to the word of God [**Psalm 102:20**].

⇒ **There is a spirit called Antichrist, which is world domination without Christ.**⇐

It is the demonic spirit behind those like Napoleon Bonaparte or Adolf Hitler who had ambition to rule the world for their glory. They try to take over the place that only belongs to God [**Psalm 24:1**].

A praying church or body can bind the demonic spirit and halt its activity.

Chapter 15
Prayer Facts

When praying there are several facts to consider, the **first** is that there is a high price to be paid in personal discipline. In other words this means that you are giving up ALL your desires to Him.

Essentially you are selling out to God and willing to be crucified with him. [**Galatians 2:20**]

When you totally give all to Him, He chooses to display His UNLIMITED power *to* and *through* you by giving us HIS authority. Now, we have been given such authority in our inheritance with the King of Kings so that we may go everywhere and preach the gospel of the kingdom.

We are priests and kings, the ambassadors of Christ [**II Cor 5:20**] who now stand in His place for the entire world to see. The authority that God has given to the believer shows that <u>nothing is impossible</u>.

<u>1 Peter 4:1, 2</u> Forasmuch then as Christ hath suffered for us in the flesh, arm yourselves likewise with the same mind: for he that hath suffered in the flesh hath ceased from sin; That he no longer should live the rest of [his] time in the flesh to the lusts of men, but to the will of God.

The **second** fact is that we are to be in constant communion with God. Prayer sets God's spiritual laws in motion.

<u>Ephesians 6:18</u> Praying always with all prayer and supplication in the Spirit, and watching thereunto with all perseverance and supplication for all saints;
<u>1 Thessalonians 5:17</u> Pray without ceasing.
<u>1 Peter 3:12</u> For the eyes of the Lord [are] over the righteous, and His ears [are open] unto their prayers.
<u>Jeremiah 33:3</u> Call unto me, and I will answer thee, and shew thee great and mighty things, which thou knowest not.
<u>Hebrews 4:16</u> Let us therefore come boldly unto the throne of grace, that we may obtain mercy, and find grace to help in time of need.

Third, to be effective in prayer, it must be based on God's Word. This kind of preparation comes from spending time in the Word of God *daily*. How can prayers be based on the Word if you do not fill yourself *with* the Word everyday?

<u>Jeremiah 1:12</u> Then said the Lord unto me, Thou hast well seen: for I will hasten my *word* to perform it.
<u>Isaiah 43:26</u> Put me in remembrance [of My Word]…
<u>Isaiah 55:11</u> So shall My *word* be that goeth forth out of My mouth: it shall not return unto me void, but it shall accomplish that which I please, and it shall prosper [in the thing] whereto I sent it.

You are God's mouthpiece!

Walking in the Supernatural Power of Prayer

Joshua 1:8 This book of the law shall not depart out of thy mouth; but thou shalt meditate therein day and night, that thou mayest observe to do according to all that is written therein: for then thou shalt make thy way prosperous, and then thou shalt have good success.

Fourth, prayer **must always** be the foundation of every Christian endeavor because what God desires for us can only be accomplished through the foundation of prayer. Any failure is a prayer failure. How can that be? **Colossians 1:9-13** shows us that God desires for His people to be successful, filled with a deep clear knowledge of His will, and bearing fruit in every good work.

Fifth, you must be specific in your prayers to get answers. Paul is an excellent example of a man who prayed specifically and prayers were answered. These examples can be found in [**Ephesians 1:16-19; 3:14-19; Philippians 1:9-11; Colossians 1:9-11; 2 Thessalonians 1:11, 12**].

Sixth, prayer can either be defensive or offensive. Basically, you can either rush around putting out fires or you can capture and sentence the one setting the fires. It is imperative you be aggressive in your prayer life to have victory everywhere else.

Finally an aspect of prayer is doing battle with the invisible forces of darkness. Prayer helps us to overcome and defeat the demons of hell assigned to hinder us [Christians]. It can destroy the enemy's power and his evil forces. And it can build the kingdom of God.

?How many times should you pray the same prayer?
Until it is fixed in your heart!

Andrew Murray said, "It is not good taste to ask God for something over and over." We should tell God we are <u>expecting answers</u> and <u>thank Him for it</u>.

?What can your prayers do?
√ Bring salvation to the sinner
√ Bring deliverance to the oppressed
√ Bring healing to the sick
√ Bring prosperity to the poor
√ Usher in the next move of God for your city, country, and the whole earth
√ Change you

<u>Confession:</u> **Let my prayers be powerful prayers that change things. God help me to pray aggressively like Moses, Elijah, Paul, and Jesus did.**

NOTES

Chapter 16
Foundations of Prayer

Is there a formula to prayer? Though prayer can be learned, there is no set formula. The disciples saw something in Christ's prayer they desired. [**Luke 11:1**] Pride can prevent us from learning more about prayer [**James 1:21**]. And being a forgetful hearer can prevent growth in prayer [**James 1:22-25**].

Prayer should come from the heart. God is more concerned about the attitude of our hearts rather than external things. [**Luke 18:10-14**] We can't lean on the works of the flesh for answered prayer.

Our entrance to the throne room of God is righteousness. It's all based on our relationship with Him. [**Luke 11:2**] Jesus' work on the cross created an entrance into the throne room for us. [**2 Corinthians 5:21**] God wants to take us on as a partner in blessing the world. [**2 Corinthians 6:1**] Being bold in prayer is something we can do because boldness is different from pride. [**Genesis 18:23-27**]

Faith is the first requirement to answered prayer and flourishes where there is strong fellowship. [**Matthew 21:22**] We must recognize the difference in the natural and spiritual worlds as well as the difference between hearsay and personal knowledge.

We should also identify the hindrances to prayers. One is unconfessed sin. It separates us from grace and creates a spiritual 'heart attack'. [**Psalm 66:18; 1 John 3:20-22**] Unforgiveness creates a spiritual barrier. Jesus distinctly made a point of connecting forgiveness and prayer. Some other hindrances are strife, selfishness, false faith and worry.

Types of Prayer

√ Prayer for those in authority
√ Prayer for the lost
√ Prayer in the Spirit

√ Prayer of faith
√ Prayer of intercession
√ United Prayer

Our Support to Prayer

♦ God's Provision
♦ The will of God

♦ The Blood Covenant

♦ Praise and Worship
The highest type of prayer
Exchanging the garment of praise for the spirit of heaviness

♦ Fasting

♦ Persistence in Prayer

♦ Spiritual Warfare

Patience is the neglected element of prayer.
Hope is the expectation of God's divine favor.

We need to understand Satan's devices.
We need to know our authority.

♦ Christ's Intercession

NOTES

Chapter 17
Supernatural Power of Prayer

Perseverance [steadfastness in doing something despite difficulty or delay in achieving success] in prayer is the path to power. Prayer to the Christian is like breath to any living thing. Therefore we need to pray and keep on praying because it crucifies the flesh and reveals the Spirit of God buried underneath.

Prayer is for spiritual growth and development. Unless we have a life of prayer we will never grow to our spiritual potential. It is the lifeline of God's spirit in our own lives. When we pray to the Father in Jesus' name, we give the Holy Spirit permission to invade our lives with Himself to: kill a little more of us (flesh), reveal more of God, and release our spirit-man in this realm. [**Matthew 7; Galatians 6:7; Mark 4:20; Romans 8:26; 1 Corinthians 14:2; Jude 19, 20; John 7:27**]

Prayer is also required for the Holy Spirit to water and help release the implanted seed of God's potential in us.

⇒**Satan's number one job is to knock us out of prayer.**⇐

He understands better than we sometimes do that as we pray we really are dangerous to him and his schemes. We are able to overcome the obstacles he places in our lives. Prayer leads us to victory!

Ironically the one area we must be the strongest in is actually the one we, the Church, are the weakest in. Can we relate to this in our personal lives? Fellowship and connection with the Father who is able to empower us in the challenges of life is so vital, especially if we are heading into, are in, or are coming out of a crisis.

⇒**What is the will of God for us? Prayer and His word is His will for us.**⇐

However, there are times His written word does not always address His specific will for our particular situation. This is where prayer will create the spiritual environment for the Holy Spirit to enlighten us to His specific will.

⇒**Without action in our lives as we pray for the will of God can be a difficult thing to perceive.**⇐

There are also times where He says to be still and know that He is God [**Psalm 46:10**]. Then not moving at all can be just as negative as never slowing down. We need the Holy Spirit's direction and we can only discern that if we pray.

Personally I make the assumption I am in the will of God as long as I am not in direct disobedience to scripture and am not grieved in my heart by the Holy Spirit [**1 John 5:14, 15**]. Christ, the Anointed One and the Hope of Glory dwells inside of me. He goes where I go unless He blows a loud spiritual alarm in my heart.

Walking in the Supernatural Power of Prayer

⇒The key to prayer is endurance⇐

Of course fifteen-minute prayer chains are good. After all, prayer is a blessing. However, praying for such a short period of time is not a long enough time for the Holy Spirit to do the work He needs to do in us. Do not misunderstand, God can do anything; however, soaking in His presence and allowing the Holy Spirit to do a deep work will affect a change within us that is so intricately and thoroughly rooted in God, the devil can neither undo it, nor deceive us in that area.

⇒Prayer is NOT moving God. WE are the ones who should be doing the moving.⇐

The method in which we pray is not the most important aspect. We should just PRAY! What stops Him is our unbelief. Is there unbelief? The answer is pray. JUST PRAY!

A lack of prayer will permit Satan to latch onto a weakness in our lives.

It's not always a frontal assault invasion, but a covert, subtle, slow, and undercover attack. Be careful because he can also preach grace to us. He will say things like: you still have God's touch on your life, don't you? He'll try and distract us by getting into non-spiritual activities like TV or games. Satan will build strongholds in our minds with these kinds of mind occupying activities.

This subtle approach of Satan will be an avenue for him to attach himself to a weakness in our lives. The strategy is to cause us to fall out of prayer. We'll go so far in consistency in our prayer life then something causes an interruption.

On the opposite end of the spectrum a life of prayer permits the Spirit to saturate us and open a pathway for His presence into our tabernacles. It also permits the Holy Spirit an ongoing access to our hearts. He is constantly searching and putting His blessed pressure on the specific and subtle strategies of Satan he uses.

Some of those strategies are an attack with guilt and unworthiness. Remember, *condemnation* is always Satan's way and *conviction* is always the Holy Spirit's way.
The ministry of the Holy Spirit is to reveal Jesus to us and in us so He will be revealed to the rest of the world.

What do we do if we fall out of consistently praying? The prescription is to enter a time of fasting and prayer. Fasting will re-establish us in prayer. Fasting with prayer will cause the death of fears, insecurities, rejections, and intimidations [the same issues Satan likes to latch on to]. When these fears, torments, and insecurities begin to die, they will be replaced by peace.

We will notice a clearer, stronger sense of the Holy Spirit's promptings in leading and guiding. This is prayer that is powerful! It also permits us to yield to the ministry of the Holy Spirit to reveal Jesus through us.

Michael Angelo had to be able to see David inside the marble first. Then he began to chisel away the excess stone with amazing precision and revealed the David hidden within. The ministry of the Holy Spirit is the same way. He removes the flesh until the Christ hidden in us is revealed.

Begin focusing on prayer and watch out for Satan. He will examine our weak areas to reveal them and bring them against us. One person's weakness may not be the same as another's. Many Christians that are moved to prayer by inspiration and revelation knowledge are willing to lay their weaknesses aside and march into prayer.

Walking in the Supernatural Power of Prayer

By reporting for prayer Satan will magnify fears and an emotional war and turmoil will begin.

Be encouraged! The Holy Spirit will move His searchlight over these areas of attack we may identify with and He will edify us in these areas [**1 Corinthians 14:3**]. We will either be purged from the sin or we'll quit praying. If we quit praying and settle down in church, ten years from now we'll find our lives are no different.

God has set up an entire process He designed to minister on the inside of us where all permanent change takes place. Enduring prayer is what brings you into a place of change and a place of power in God.

Moses was given a place beside God on Mt. Sinai [**Deuteronomy 5:20**]. It is a place of relationship, power, God's presence, and worship. **Paul Yonggi Ch**o's mother-in-law spent ten years of enduring prayer for him. It has resulted in the largest church in the world since the church of Ephesus when Timothy pastured there.

Persistent prayer will do what nothing else can do. God is not mocked, be not deceived for whatsoever a man soweth that shall he also reap [**Galatians 6:7**]. If we stay in prayer long enough we will get addicted and Satan will have to deal with us at some point. That's why he'd rather deal with us now before we are someone to be reckoned with. After all, many are called but few are chosen [**Matthew 22:14**].

Jesus teaches us how to pray in [**Matthew 6:8-15**]. And He gives further instructions in [**Matthew 7:7, 8**]. If we are persistent in asking, it shall be given to us. If we keep earnestly seeking, it shall be found by us. And if we keep reverently knocking, the door shall be opened to us. God's desire is to see us receive of Him and that the desire for self-glorification dies. When this happens the life of God comes forth.

NOTES

Chapter 18
Endurance in Prayer UNTIL the Answer Comes

⇒The word **endurance** means **continuance** or a state of lasting or duration without yielding to pressure, resistance, pain or distress. Endurance in prayer despite Satan's tactics has a variety of advantages. First and foremost it opens the door to revelatory knowledge of the Word of God and that is power.

In [**Mark 4:2-25**] Jesus speaks a parable of the seed and the sower. The seed sown is the Word of God and the objective of the parable is to produce a hundred fold or rather His perfect will. The Word of God is the candle given to us to illuminate anything in our lives that would keep us from producing the hundred fold.

The Word guards us against persecutions, afflictions and cares of this life, the deceitfulness of riches, and the lust for other things of this world. As the candlestick was to light the Holy Place in the Tabernacle so is the Word of God designed to shine a light on that which hinders us from entering into God's perfect will. [**Matthew 10:26, 27; John 1:5**]

Not only does **Mark 4** speak of revelation knowledge about personal hindrances but also about how to use the Word to move 'the mountain' [**Mark 11:23, 24**] God gave us the Word and the most powerful way to ignite the candle is to permit the Holy Spirit in our lives on a personal level. We do this by meditating on the Word of God and praying in the Holy Spirit.

The majority of 'good' churches do not know how to activate the word in their lives. How tragic! How long have we heard the Word ministered or sown in our hearts? What has kept us from producing the 30 – 60 – 100 fold return?

⇒**Endurance in prayer is praying in the Holy Spirit and praying the Word.**⇐

Doing this keeps our focus sharp. We'll speak divine secrets from the Word and the Word within us will begin to ignite and reveal the obstacles that keep us from receiving God in these areas. [**1 Corinthians 14:2, 4a, 13-15, 18, 21**] Praying in the Holy Spirit [**Jude 19, 20**] will help us to 'contend for the faith' [**Jude 3**]. Our lives will transition from regular 'churchianity' to anointed ministry no matter what our call is.

When the Holy Ghost begins to light the candle of our knowledge, the strength for "mortification" comes and the areas of weakness exposed by His light are put to death. [**Colossians 3:1-10; Romans 8:10, 11; Luke 11:33-36**]

⇒**Jesus created a model for prayer to approach the Father.**⇐

Jesus created a model for prayer to approach the Father [**Luke11:1-4**]. As he taught us how to pray, He also taught us how to pray on behalf of another (intercession) [**Luke 11:5-9**]. After He taught us how to pray, he encouraged persistence (**endurance**) in our praying [**Luke 11:9, 10**]. He knew we'd need persistence because we may be fighting spiritual darkness in the heavenlies, or fighting the flesh along with the spiritual forces.

Walking in the Supernatural Power of Prayer

Our spirit is the candle (light bulb) of the Lord. [**Proverbs 20:27**] It is the part of us created in God's image which the Holy Spirit ignites to illuminate my understanding of Him and imparting revelation knowledge to me. [**Luke 11:36**] tells us that our whole body should be full of light since we walk in the light.

It is the Holy Spirit, the light of Truth, who searches out all the inward parts and shines the light on any dark places. This searching process takes place in us as we pray in tongues [**1 Corinthians 14:3, 4, 18, 39**]. The ministry of the Holy Spirit is to help bring us into the image of His Son. [**Romans 8:26-30**] He teaches us the things we cannot discern and shows us mysteries and divine secrets we need to know about God and His ways. If we permit the Holy Spirit to teach us, He will reveal God's plan for us.

When we pray in an unknown tongue, we aren't speaking to men. We are speaking to God and actually edifying ourselves. Edify comes from the word edifice. In a sense we are erecting a superstructure on the inside of our spirits to house the anointing of God and to qualify us for our divine calling. We are in a spirit-to-spirit communication with God. [**1 Corinthians 14:2**]

This enduring prayer is where we present our bodies as a living sacrifice unto God [**Jude 20, 21**].

⇒**The power of the early church came from their personal prayer life and intimacy with God.**⇐

People were healed through Paul's handkerchiefs and Peter's shadow. However, there were some that once walked in the power but darkness put out their light. Jude calls these men "raging waves of the sea, foaming out their own shame; wandering stars to whom is reserved the blackness of darkness forever." [**Jude 13**]

[**Jude 12**] calls these men 'clouds without water', full of promise without delivery. Clouds should have water to give needed rain. The doctrines of man stole their power and the church was plunged into the "dark ages". She lost her faith for hundreds of years.

[**Jude 19**] says, "these by they who separate themselves, sensual, having not the Spirit." Carnal appetites of the flesh dominated them rather than God's word and His Spirit. The Holy Spirit was NOT in operation; therefore, there was no light, only darkness.

⇒ *Isn't being baptized in the Holy Spirit enough?* ⇐

If we have the Holy Spirit, we should build ourselves up in our most holy faith. We need to build ourselves up above a walk dominated by the senses. This is why we need to pray in the Holy Ghost. Being edified [**Jude 20**] delivers us from the strife-filled, carnal condition described in [**Jude 19**] and enables us to live continually in [**Jude 21**].

NOTES

Chapter 19
Dismantling the Enemy's Activity By Intercessory Prayer

⇒ In intercessory prayer, the one praying commands the devil to stop his activity so that the will of God can be fulfilled.

⇒ Satan stands against God's promises and binds people today. He binds the demonic powers like alcohol, depression, and anger which are holding a person in bondage.

⇒ During intercessory prayer we will pray in our **prayer language** most of the time.

An intercessor is someone who pulls two that have been separated back together again. For better understanding imagine four different persons: GOD, MAN, DEVIL, and the INTERCESSOR. The devil has his arms around the man and is pulling him away from God. Though the man tries to reach out for God, he is unable to reach Him because the man is bound by the devil. The intercessor first breaks the bonds of the devil (breaking the hold around the man's waist) and then joins the man with God (representing his will joining God's will).

Matthew 9:35, 36 show us that the basis for Jesus' ministry was love and compassion for all mankind. It never said that He took pity on someone. Likewise the basis for intercessor prayer is love and compassion. Compassion goes further than pity. Both express sorrow for the suffering of others; however, compassion acts to do something about it spiritually.

Steps of Intercessory Prayer

- **Go Through the Gates:** In the Bible the gate stands for authority. It is at the city gates where the authority of the city sat and ruled. Satan is the father of all unbelievers and the authority over everything on earth. When we pray a prayer of intercession, we go past the authority holding the person from coming to the Lord. "…And the gates of hell shall not prevail against (the church)" – [**Matthew 16:18**]

- **Prepare the Way of the People; Cast (Build) up the Highway:** In a prayer of intercession we prepare the way for the people to come to God through salvation by building up a highway in the spirit. We plow the 'hard ground' by praying in tongues. We 'build the highway' by speaking the promises of salvation found in the Bible [**Acts 16:31; 2 Peter 3:9**] "The voice of him that crieth in the wilderness, Prepare ye the way of the Lord, make straight in the desert a highway for our God." – [**Isaiah 40:3**]

- **Gather (Cast) Out the Stones:** We pray the hindrances from the person's life that would keep them from coming to the Lord like fear, unbelief, unworthiness, and false doctrine.

- **Lift up a Standard:** Teach them God's word

Intercessory prayer is a prayer of persistence.

[**Luke 11:5-13**] is a Biblical example of the prayer of intercession. We find in verse 9 that if we ask we will receive. Therefore, keep on asking, seeking, and knocking. It is not just a prayer of petition because this kind of praying involves another's will who has been deceived by and bound by Satan and strongholds have built up as a result.

Persistence is a strong, shameless stand on the word of God.

We will **NOT** look at the circumstances or what the person is doing. We will look at God's promises instead and believe them no matter what it looks like. We are going to continue to persist against the gates of hell until the answer comes. And we will take authority over the spiritual forces that are controlling the person's life.

NOTES

Chapter 20
Biblical Examples of Powerful Prayer

The Bible gives several examples of prayer so powerful it changed lives and the courses of events. Jesus Christ was our ultimate example when it came to praying. Even on the night He was betrayed His prayer was for His disciples and the work He came to do.

~JESUS~

In [**John 17**] Jesus said, "Glorify Me so that I may give eternal life. I have glorified You (God) here on earth by completing the work You gave Me to do. Restore Me to the majesty and honor in Your presence, as I had with You before the world existed. I have revealed Your real self to the people you have given me out of the world."

He had completed the work God had for Him to do and now was the pivotal moment when sin would forever be covered by His blood. He would be resurrected and all would know Him as Jesus the Messiah. Now the disciples are convinced God sent Jesus and they understand all God has given to Jesus belongs to God.

Jesus said, "I am not praying for the world, but for those You have given Me for they belong to You." Jesus wasn't talking about creation but His children, those that belonged to Him. It is through His children that His glory is achieved.

He tells His Father, "I am coming to You. Keep in the knowledge of Yourself those whom You have given Me (the church) that they may be one (unity) as we are one (spiritual unity). Let My job be made complete in them that they may have My joy within them filling their hearts."

He prayed for His disciple's protection. "I do not ask that You take them out of the world but that you protect and keep them from the evil one and that they live above the evil of this world. Sanctify (separate) them for Yourself and make them holy. Just as You sent Me into the world, I also have sent them into the world."

He didn't leave out His future children. He was looking ahead at the generations to come. "Not just for the disciples who follow Me now do I pray but also for all those who will ever come to believe in Me through their word. I pray they all may be one in Us so that the world may believe and be convinced You have sent Me and so that they may be perfectly united (spiritually)."

H reaffirmed that He completed the work by saying, "I made Your name known and revealed Your character and I will continue to make You known that the love which You have bestowed upon Me may be in them and that I may be in them."

~PETER and JOHN with fellow BELIEVERS~

In **Acts 4** Peter and John were imprisoned for preaching and doing miracles. After they were questioned, they were threatened not to preach or teach in the name of Jesus and they were released. Then they went to the believers and shared with them all that had happened. When everyone heard about it, they lifted up their voice to God, with one accord, and said, "Lord, Thou [art] God, which hast made heaven, and earth, and the sea, and all that in them is:" [**Acts 4:24**]

Walking in the Supernatural Power of Prayer

Acts 4:29-31 And now, Lord, behold their threatenings: and grant unto thy servants, that with all boldness (confidence) they may speak they word, by stretching forth thine hand to heal; and that signs and wonders may be done by the name of the holy child, Jesus. And when they had prayed, the place was shaken where they were assembled together; and they were all filled with the Holy Ghost, and they spake the word of God with boldness [not a natural boldness].

~HOME of MARY, mother of JOHN MARK~

In **Acts 12** Herod, the king, began persecuting the Church. He killed James, the disciple of Jesus, and imprisoned Peter. Fervent prayer was made without ceasing by the church unto God for him [**Acts 12:5**].

The night before Herod was going to sentence Peter to death, Peter was asleep between two soldiers and fastened with chains. He also had guards sitting before the door of the prison cell guarding it. Suddenly an angel appeared beside Peter and told him to get up. Immediately the chains fell off his hands and Peter followed the angel to the outside of the prison.

Peter came to the house of Mary the mother of John, whose surname was Mark: where many were gathered together praying [**Acts 12:12**]. Once inside, Peter related to them about His deliverance.

~ELIJAH~

James 5:16b-18 The earnest (heartfelt, continued) prayer of a righteous man makes tremendous power available [dynamic in its working]. (*James 5:16b Amplified Version*)
Elias was a man subject to like passions as we are, and he prayed earnestly that it might not rain: and it rained not on the earth by the space of three years and six months. And he prayed again, and the heaven gave rain, and the earth brought forth her fruit.

The Israelites had been worshiping false gods and they were in sin. The word says in Deuteronomy that if they worshiped false gods, they would be cursed with drought. If they repented, it would rain. Their sin did opened the way for Elijah to pray the way he did and he was obedient to pray the way God told him to.

~CORNELIUS~

In **Acts 10** Cornelius got his whole family to pray together. The prayer brought Peter 160 kilometers to preach to them. They all received the baptism of the Holy Spirit.

~PAUL~

There are also some powerful prayers that Paul prayed found in [**Ephesians 1:16-19; 3:14-19; Philippians 1:9-11; Colossians 1:9-11; 2 Thessalonians 1:11, 12**].

NOTES

Chapter 21
Inviting the Holy Spirit to be Our Guide in Prayer

As believers we simply must know how to pray but let's invite the Holy Spirit to be our guide and comforter.

[**Jude 1:20**] We must pray in the **Holy Ghost** and build ourselves up in our most holy faith. Doing this will help us withstand what the Lord Jesus has warned us about in [**Matthew 24:4-13**] Praying in the Spirit greatly helps to build us up in our faith. When we don't know what to pray for, the Spirit will help us pray. He prays in an unknown language, praying for our needs when we don't even know them yet [**Romans 8:26-27**].

Fully trust the Lord …keep yourselves in the love of God, waiting for the mercy of our Lord Jesus Christ that leads to eternal life [**Jude 21**]. [**Proverbs 3:5**] reminds us to "trust in the Lord with all your heart; do not depend on your own understanding." *And we must know the word of God to speak it in prayer.*

> ➤ **When praying we must be specific and stand on God's promises.**

Many times we are not clear in what we want when we pray. To receive an answer to our prayers we must decide what we want from God and find the scripture or scriptures that definitely promises us these things. > Be Single Minded

Pray according to God's word. Too few Christians realize the importance of the word of God in prayer. God's word is His will; therefore, we need to find scriptures that promise the things we are asking for. His word will not come back void.

Many Christians cannot pray in **confidence and boldness** because they do not know God's promises. Once we find the scriptures that show God's promise, we must get them in our hearts as well as in our minds. For example, if we are looking for God to heal, we should get familiar with these scriptures and pray them each to God: [**Isaiah 53:4, 5; Matthew 8:17; 1 Peter 2:24**]

Use the sword (word) against the enemy. Follow Jesus' example as He use the word against the enemy in [**Matthew 4:1-11**]. Fight the good fight: [**1 Timothy 6:12**]. We must stand on God's promises and worship!

> ➤ **We must ask God for what we want.**
> <u>Isaiah 55:11</u> **NIV** so is my word that goes out from my mouth: It will not return to me empty, but will accomplish what I desire and achieve the purpose for which I sent it.

To receive what we want is to ask God what we want then believe we will receive them [**Matthew 6:33; John 16:23, 24; Matthew 7:7, 8; Mark 11:23, 24**]

Do not let sense knowledge override revelation truth. The mind is at war with your spirit and must be brought under the control of the Holy Spirit. [**Ephesians 1:3; Romans 3:4**]

Walking in the Supernatural Power of Prayer

> ➤ **Let every thought and desire affirm that we have what we ask for.
> We are to be positive in our thinking.**

Once we have prayed and asked God for something, we are to never permit a negative picture of failure to remain in our minds.

Counter all negative thoughts with God's promise and word. We must resist doubt and rebuke it. Doubt is from Satan. We must get our mind on the word of God, which is our answer.

All images, thoughts, suggestions, visions, dreams, impressions, and feelings that do not contribute to our faith must be completely removed from our minds.
Reject anything that contradicts the word: [**Matthew 8:17; Hebrews 1:1, 2**]. It is not enough to feel that God has heard our prayers. We must believe and know for a surety that He has heard our prayers.

> ➤ **We are to guard our mind against any evil thought that comes to try and get us to doubt God's word.**

The Bible tells us in Philippians what to think on. We must guard our minds in order to develop faith. As we stand our ground and remain firm in faith, our faith will see us through to victory. [**Philippians 4:8; 2 Corinthians 10:5**]

> ➤ **We must meditate on God's words and promises.**

We must see ourselves in possession of what we have asked God for [**Proverbs 4:20-22**]. If a loved one needs healing we should meditate on [**Matthew 8:17 and Isaiah 53:5**]. We need to see ourselves with our answers [**John 15:7**]. We ask what we will and it shall be done unto us.

> ➤ **Continually thank God for the answer. [Philippians 4:6]**

> ➤ **Make every prayer a statement of faith.**

It is thinking faith thoughts and speaking faith words which leads the heart out of defeat and into victory. Do not let your heart condemn you

Andrew Murray said, "*It is not good taste to ask God for something over and over.*" We should tell God we are expecting answers and thank Him for it.

Let us **not** undo our prayers. We should use the **faith** we have [**Romans 12:3**].

NOTES

Chapter 22
Praying For Your Town, City, and Country

Proclamation: "Arise oh gates and lift up your heads everlasting doors, and the King of glory shall come in. Who is this King of Glory? The Lord strong and mighty; the Lord mighty in battle. Arise oh gates and lift up your heads everlasting doors, and the King of glory shall come in. Who is this King of glory? The Lord of hosts: He is the King of glory, Selah." [**Psalm 24:7-10**]

Job 12:23 He makes nations great and destroys them: He enlarges nations, and disperses them.

As believers we can have an influence over our city, country, government etc.. We must study God's strategy (the Word) so that we will be ready to cooperate with the Holy Spirit; ready to be obedient when He is ready to move. Ask God how we can take our city and country with the Gospel. Keeping our focus on God's position, purpose and plans for our city and country will help us believe.

We need to confess the sins of our country and ask God to have mercy on His people and to revive His work in our city and country. [**Habakkuk 3:2**] We pray for God to unite the body of Christ and to convict His people of pride and prejudice that separates them. The church needs to realize that without unity they will not make it.

Matthew 12:25 Every kingdom divided against itself is brought to desolation; and every city or house divided against itself shall not stand.

Intercessors worldwide need to RISE UP. Empowered by the Holy Spirit they need to pray for their country on a regular basis. [Psalm 2:8]

We should pray that our hearts and minds are toward the unsaved in our city and country. [**2 Peter 3:9**] Ask God for visionaries who will seek God for strategies of how to reach the unevangelized and to put laborers into the harvest fields. Target the prayers towards the youth and children because Satan targets them. [**Proverbs 29:18; Matthew 9:37, 38**]

We can pray **specifically** for our city because a battle is raging over the city and it affects us right now. And seek the peace of the city…and pray to the Lord for it: for in its peace you will have peace. [**Jeremiah 29:7**]

Our individual blind spots and vices are usually common to the culture around us

And principalities and powers influence these deficiencies. Spiritual warfare for our city begins on a personal level; expands to our families, our church, the corporate church, the nation and finally the world.

We can determine our city's redemptive gift. God has participated in the creation of every city, both in forming its personality and in stationing angels over each one, like Michael, the archangel, is the defender of Israel. [**Daniel 10**] Determining our city's redemptive gift is more important than discerning the nature of evil principalities. The principalities are what pervert the gift.

Country	Redemptive Gift	Satan's Perversion
New York City	Gateway of hope to a land of liberty	Today it is known for greed, ruthlessness and despair
Amsterdam	Tradition of hospitality and tolerance; city of refuge	Today it is known for tolerance to open drug trade and legalized prostitution
Jerusalem	Peace and praise	Today it is known as a place of conflict where God's character is continually misrepresented through religious conflict

Demonic powers have infested the earth's atmosphere since before the creation of mankind, but they can only extend their authority into a town when people sin. Therefore, we need to ask the question: is there anything in the root of our city that would be bringing God's judgment rather than His blessing?

2 Chronicles 34:27 Judgment has already been declared and is inevitable, but you can turn to God in humility and He will revive you and your children with you.

- We should ask God to reveal the spiritual nature and/or type of oppression in our city and to reveal the principalities and powers that are over it and pray for their influence to be bound. God will reveal what we need to know when we need to know it. Our prayer should be the same as [**Isaiah 64:1-3**].

Isaiah 64:1-3 Oh that thou wouldest rend the heavens, that thou wouldest come down, that the mountains might flow down at they presence, as [when] the melting fire burneth, the fire causeth the waters to boil, to make thy name known to thine adversaries, [that] the nations may tremble at thy presence! When thou didst terrible things [which] we looked not for, thou camest down, the mountains flowed down at they presence.

One of the best things we can do is find out the history of the church in our country and city. Discover where the spiritual walls of our city have broken down. It may be that our forefathers received promises from for the city that has never been fulfilled.

Walking in the Supernatural Power of Prayer

Good News! There are steps towards victory.

➢ Worship! It is in the place of thanksgiving that God produces within us His mind and heart for our city.

➢ Wait on God for insight; do NOT rely on human reasoning or go by emotions.

➢ Spiritual battles are won by following revelation given by the Holy Spirit.

➢ Identify with the sins of the city [**Nehemiah 1:6**] Great intercessors of the Bible did not come into the presence of God to cover up sin but to agree with His assessment of it. They approached God with a sense of shame and embarrassment. They were willing to face with honesty the wickedness of the culture around them. Humility and honest are the keys to effective prayer

➢ Overcome evil with good. When we discern an activity of a principality with a particular characteristic, you need to fight with the opposite characteristic, not only through resisting the temptation but also by demonstrating the positive action. For example, fight lust with purity, lethargy with diligence, greed with generosity, fear with faith, and pride with humility.

The Gospel reveals a message of **faith, hope, and love.** Faith is receiving the knowledge of God's ability and character. Hope is the expectation of His goodness to us. And love is the experience of intimate affection; His grace poured out. The promise of the Gospel is realized only as we identify with Christ (our Great Intercessor) and His ongoing labor of prayer.

God has given us the ability to move in a realm of the Spirit where "nothing is impossible." He has given us every dimension of His power, might and strength.

**The most difficult part is our willingness to believe that all heaven now backs us
AND the spirit of Christ lives with in US!**

God has freely given us this unimaginable blessing and gift – the life and authority of Christ! If we are going to grow and develop into the fullness of the ministry of Jesus, there must be a complete surrender and consecration to His will. We must give ourselves over entirely to the mentorship of the Holy Spirit who will lead us and guide us.

The Holy Spirit will teach us how to do the works of Jesus just like He did them. He will train us in all the conduct and manner of His life. Through the training and guidance of the Spirit, the power of God will flow through us with the demonstration of great wonders and miracles; every yoke will be broken and every criminal of hell stopped!

**Reference: Read the manual 'The Secret Names of the Strongman'
that hinder your cit**

Before YOU Go Out and Pray

Bind your opponent with the word using the name of Jesus

[Mark 3:27] In fact, no one can enter a strong mans house without binding him.

~ Serious Notes for Warfare ~

1. Do not go before God sends you

2. Remember the battle is God's, not yours. Ask God to send out his warring angels.

3. Unity and prayer keeps one another strong

4. Repent of any unforgiveness you may towards anyone including yourself and God. The spirit of **Rabisu (serpent)** is looking for a crack in your armor.

5. If anyone who is a reasoner and not spiritual and NOT being spirit led of the spirit :**Ask for help.**

6. Leave religion behind and hold on to relationship with God. That is where your strength is

7. Ask him to go before you as a great shield of faith to quench the fiery darts of the adversary.

Walking in the Supernatural Power of Prayer

~ Prayer For the Group to be said Out Loud Together ~

Lord, thank you for being my covering and strong tower. Thank you that you hide me from the adversary and his allies and anyone who would harm me in any way whether spiritually, emotionally, physically, materialistically and financially.

Thank you that you protect me from slander, lies, soul ties, false accusations, deformation of character, hate and jealousy and all the powers of the enemy.

Thank you that you protect me from the wicked and the prayers of the self righteous immature Christians of control, charismatic witchcraft, dambala, voodoo and witchcraft.

I take this spring equinox time seriously and see how it births. I wrap the deceived and wicked ones in the word of God and bind up and arrest all thoughts, words and deeds of plans that will bring destruction and cause their kingdom to grow any further. I bind the ways and thoughts of man who follow after Satan with the spirit of ISIS and ask that the spirit of chaos will be loosed now to ALL of them. BREAK their strategies and cause their timeframe of Satan and religious ways to be disrupted so the anti-christ spirit cannot continue to flourish in the land which binds up the hearts, spirit and minds of men which keeps them from accepting you as Lord and Savior. I come against their stubborn and rebellious spirit and ask that our prayers will loose them to the cross of Calvary.

Their agenda is to possess the land and we ask now that you loose your warring angels to begin fighting upon our behalf as your ambassadors. He who the son sets free his free indeed. We ask that YOU come as the Lion of the tribe of Judah and face down the Kingdoms, their leaders and underlings that have been established in countries and in the USA.

We are your intercessors and we stand up as prophets and speak to the prince and powers of the air and against principalities in high places and command their ways to be bound. In their place we loose the power of the Holy Spirit to go and find out what is hidden that needs to be destroyed.

Father I ask that you will take them down under the bowels of the earth and keep them there until the day of judgment. For those leaders who will not obey you and continue with a hard heart and unwillingness to come to you, remove them the way you desire.

We pray for ALL political leaders especially who are joined in the listing above and in the occult ways that that you change their ways we command them to be powerless. We arrest all their thoughts, words and deeds of plans that will bring destruction and cause their kingdom not to grow. We wrap them in the word of God and command them to listen to the Holy Spirit...You will obey God's voice and be a blessing for his kingdom and his people.

Seeking the Welfare of the Communities

A bitter, hard prayer

In[**Psalm 137**] the psalmist reacts negatively to an attempt on the part of one of his Babylonian captors to get him to sing one of the songs of Jerusalem. The bitterness and sorrow expressed in that psalm capture what must have been the heart burden of many of the people of Israel, as they endured captivity in Babylon. How could they sing the Lord's songs in a foreign land? How could they even think of letting the cruel Babylonians gain any benefit from their devotions?

And yet [**Psalm 137**], bitter and hard as it is, is a prayer to God. It's what we call an imprecatory psalm, calling the judgment of God down against those who harm His people.

God commanded His exiled people to pray for their captors; doubtless such imprecatory prayers often arose from the midst of the captive people. And God approved them, understanding and compassionate with His people all the way.

>>Seeking God's grace

But the people of God must not stop here. Even as they sought the Lord's vengeance against their captors, the exiles in Babylon were commanded also to seek His grace on their behalf, that He might penetrate their hearts, turning many to the knowledge of God. Asaph had shown the way for such prayer in [**Psalm 83:16**].

The people must also pray, as Daniel doubtless did for King Nebuchadnezzar, that their captors would repent of their violent and oppressive ways and learn to worship the living God. Such prayers must have seemed like long shots for those who prayed them, but, given the experience of Nebuchadnezzar himself, we can believe that many Babylonians came to know the Lord as a result.

Seeking the welfare of the communities in which we live will be more effective when we bathe and envelop all our endeavors in prayer. Paul commanded that prayers and intercessions be made for all people everywhere [**1 Tim. 2:1, 2**]. That surely includes the people in our communities, the teachers in our schools, those who own the businesses and farms, the civil magistrates, those who defend our nation at home and abroad, and all our neighbors, associates, and coworkers.

God works through prayer, and if we wish to see the blessings of God come to the people in our communities, then we shall have to begin praying for them more earnestly.

Walking in the Supernatural Power of Prayer

>>Pray everywhere

In our private devotions, before family dinners, in our churches and Bible study groups, where two or three believers are gathered for lunch or any other reason, let prayers ascend on behalf of our neighbors. The more we pray for people, the more we will be aware of them and their needs. The more attentive we are to them, the greater is the likelihood that we will begin to reach out to them with the blessings of God.

Prayer for our communities and our nation can unite churches across denominational divides, bring pastors together on behalf their community without jealousy or suspicion, and create a united voice for revival, renewal, and awakening for the entire world.

Will we pray for our neighbors, our community, our nation, and our world? If we will not, then we must face up to the fact that we are disobeying a divine mandate, abandoning our neighbors to their folly, and stoking the fires of indifference – if not outright scorn – for the unbelieving world around.

But if we will pray, who knows what God might be willing to do?

Reference: Read the manual '<u>The Secret Names of the Strongman</u>' that hinder your city

NOTES

Chapter 23
Encourage Yourself Confessions

1. [**Colossians 1:13**] – Who hath delivered us from the power of darkness, and hath translated us into the kingdom of His dear Son.

Confession: I walk in your Godly Kingdom today, for Jesus has destroyed Satan's kingdom in my life. Satan, I command you to stop your maneuvers in my life. I bind you and cast you out

2. [**2 Corinthians 2:14**] -Now thanks be unto God, which always causeth us to triumph in Christ, and maketh manifest the savour of his knowledge by us in every place.

Confession: I walk in total triumph in every situation, for Jesus has destroyed failure in my life. I am an overcomer and can do all things through Christ. I have the victory and the victory has me! I am a victor and a king! [**Phil. 4:13; I John 5:4**]

3. [**Ephesians 2:6**] – And hath raised us up together, and made us sit together in heavenly places in Christ Jesus.

Confession: I reign from my heavenly throne-room position, for Jesus has destroyed an inferior position in my life. I rule and reign with Jesus today. Greater is He that is in me, than he that is in the world. Father, you are Lord of heaven and earth, and we go out and possess the land today. Satan's doors are closed, and many doors are open for me to speak Your Word boldly. [**I John 4:4; Luke 10:21; Josh. 1**]

4. [**II Timothy 1:7**] – For God hath not given us the spirit of fear; but of power, and of love, and of a sound mind.

Confession: I walk in soundness of mind and divine direction, for Jesus has destroyed confusion in my life. I identify with Christ's mind. I have the mind of Christ. I will not listen to the voice of doubt and discouragement. [**I Cor. 2:16; John 10:5; Josh.1**]

5. [**I Peter 2:24**] – Who His own self bare our sins in His own body on the tree, that we, being dead to sins, should live unto righteousness: by whose stripes ye were healed.

Confession: I walk in divine health, for Jesus has conquered sickness in my life. I walk in divine health and divine life, because I have the divine nature. Jesus took all my sickness upon His body, and by suffering, I am healed. Divine health pulsates through every cell of my body everyday. Sickness and disease can not, and will not latch itself to my body. [**II Peter 1:4; Matt. 8:17**]

6. [**Philippians 4:19**] – But my God shall supply all your need according to His riches in glory by Christ Jesus.

Confession: I walk in financial abundance . God supplies all of my needs – not half of them – ALL of them. Satan, take your hands off of my finances. Finances, I command you to be loosed from the world system, and placed at my account today, so I can do the work of the Lord.

7. [**Luke 4:18**] – The Spirit of the Lord is upon me, because He hath anointed me to preach the gospel to the poor; he hath sent me to heal the brokenhearted, to preach deliverance to the captives, and recovery of sight to the blind, to set at liberty them that are bruised.

Confession: Father, your anointing is on me today. It breaks yokes off the oppressed, causes blind eyes to see, deaf ears to hear, hearts to open and understand. It causes the sick to be healed, needs to be met, and it draws full attention to Your Word. Father, Your Word is alive in me today! Revelation knowledge flows out of me every day. I operate in the gifts of the Spirit as the Spirit wills today. (Isaiah 61; I Cor. 12)

8. [**Psalm 91:7**] – A thousand shall fall at thy side, and ten thousand at thy right hand; but it shall not come nigh thee.

Confession: I walk in safety and supernatural protection today. Even though a thousand fall at my side and ten thousand at my right hand, it shall not come near me. No weapon that the enemy forms against me today shall prosper. Nothing shall by any means hurt me today. [**Isaiah 54:17; Luke 10:19**]

9. [**I Peter 5:7**] – Casting all your care upon Him; for He careth for you.

Walking in the Supernatural Power of Prayer

Confession: I walk in faith today, for Jesus has taken away fear and doubt in my life. Fear will not rule me – Faith Will! Whatever is not of faith is sin, so I speak words of life. Today, I cast all my cares on Christ today. I will go throughout my day worry free. I choose to meditate on the promises, and not the problem. As I cast my cares on Christ today I will magnify God's Word in all that I do.

10. [**John 6:63**] – It is the spirit that quickeneth; the flesh profiteth nothing: the words that I speak unto you, they are spirit, and they are life.

Confession: I will speak life today for Jesus has destroyed a murmuring and complaining tongue in my life. My tongue will speak forth words of life today. My words will produce spiritual life in the hearts of men and women.

~Confession – Walking In Love~

Speak this out of your mouth. Sow this in your heart and build it into your walk.

- I am born of God. [**1 John 5:1**] I am a child of God. [**John 1:12**]

- The love of God is shed abroad in my heart by the Holy Ghost. [**Rom 5:5**]

- I walk in the light as He is in the light. [**1 John 1:7**]

- I walk in love as He walks in love. [**1 John 4:7**]

- I am rooted and grounded in love. [**Eph 3:17**]

- I speak the truth in love. [**Eph 4:15**]

- I endure long and I am patient and kind.

- I am never envious, nor do I boil over with jealousy.

- I am not boastful, nor do I display myself haughtily, or in an arrogant way. I am not inflated with pride.

- I am not rude or unmannerly.

- I am not self-seeking or insisting on my own rights or way.

- I am not touchy, fretful, or resentful.

- I take no account of the evil done to me, and I pay no attention to a suffered wrong.

- I do not rejoice at injustice and unrighteousness, but I rejoice when righteousness and truth prevail.

- I bear up under anything. I have love's strength. I have love's power.

- I am ready to believe the best of every person. My faith is not in them but in God's love.

- My hopes are fadeless under all circumstances and I endure everything without weakening.

- I never fail, become obsolete, or come to an end. [**1 Cor 13:4-7**]

~ Confession – Healing ~

Speak this out of your mouth. Sow this in your heart and build it into your walk.

- Surely Jesus has borne my sickness and carried my pains, He was esteemed stricken and smitten of God and afflicted. He was wounded for my transgressions; He was bruised for my iniquities. The chastisement of my peace was upon Him and with His stripes, I AM healed. **[Is 53:4 & 5]**

- Jesus paid the price for my healing. He bought my healing on the Cross. I will not allow my healing to be stolen from Him.

- Who His own self bare my sins in His own body on the tree, that I being dead to sin should live unto righteousness, and by whose stripes I was healed. [**1 Pet 2:24**]

- Thank you Jesus. You redeemed me from the curse of the law, because it is written, "Christ has redeemed me from the curse of the law being made a curse for me, for it, It was written, cursed is everyone that hangs on a tree." [**Gal 3:13**]

Walking in the Supernatural Power of Prayer

- "For the eyes of the Lord run to and fro throughout the whole earth to show Himself strong on behalf of them whose heart is perfect toward Him." Father, look no further. **[2 Chron 16:9]**

- "Bless the Lord O my soul, forget not all His benefits. Who forgives all thine iniquities, who heals all thy diseases." **[Ps 103:2-3]**

- "He sent His Word and healed them and delivered them from all their destructions." **[Ps 107:20]**

- "So shall My Word be that goes forth out of My mouth, it shall not return to Me void, it will accomplish that which I please and it shall prosper in the thing wherein to I sent it." **[Is 55:11]**

- "How God anointed Jesus of Nazareth with the Holy Ghost and with power, who went about doing good and healing all who were oppressed of the devil, for God was with Him." [Acts 10:38]

- "Jesus Christ the same, yesterday, today, and forever." **[Heb 13:8]**

- "Beloved, I wish above all things that you may prosper and be in health even as your soul prospers."**[3 John 2]**

- "Verily I say unto you, whosoever shall say to this mountain, be thou removed and be thou cast into the sea, and shall not doubt in his heart, but shall believe that those things which he saith shall come to pass, he shall have whatsoever he saith. Therefore I say unto you, what things whatsoever you desire, when you pray, believe that you receive them and you shall have them."**[Mark 11:23-24]**

- Thank you Jesus, according to [**Romans 8:11**], the same Spirit that raised You from the dead is dwelling within me now to quicken (make alive) my mortal body by the Holy Spirit that dwells within me. I believe that you are quickening me now.

- I thank you Jesus, I loose the resurrection and healing power working within me now, rebuilding, repairing, and restoring any damage that was done. I loose the resurrection and healing power of the Holy Spirit upon my mind, my emotions, and my body in the name of Jesus.

SPEAK OUT

Your specific problem in conjunction with this confession claiming healing & deliverance

- ❖ Thank you Jesus, that according to [**Mark 16:18**], hands have been laid on me and I believe that I have received healing power and I am now recovering. I am in my recovery period, being rebuilt, repaired, and restored to health.

- ❖ I thank you Jesus, that according to [**Psalm 118:17**], I shall not die but live, and declare Your works O Lord. The spirit of death cannot have any way in me. (List any areas you need to stand against)

~Confession – Walking In Victory~

Speak this out of your mouth. Sow this in your heart and build it into your walk.

- ❖ Whatever is born of God overcomes the world. I am born of God and I overcome the world. This is the victory that overcomes the world, even my faith. [**1 John 5:4**]

- ❖ I want to thank You God that You always cause me to triumph in Christ. [**2 Cor 2:14**]

- ❖ And I want to thank You God for giving me the victory through my Lord Jesus Christ. [**1 Cor 15:57**]

- ❖ I thank You Jesus that You are my Savior, that You are my baptizer in the Holy Spirit, that you are my Healer, that you are my Deliverer, and the Provider for all my needs.

- ❖ I thank You Jesus that I am free, no longer in bondage or slavery to anything or anyone. I am no longer a victim, but a victor!

- ❖ Thank You Jesus that according to [**John 8:36**], I AM FREE! And whom the Son sets free is FREE INDEED!

- ❖ I am not stuck in my life but I am growing and moving and changing. I am free to grow in God. I am growing in Him everyday.

- ❖ Thank You Jesus that I am free from the following:

√ I am free from all generational curses, known and unknown.
√ I am free from witchcraft, psychic powers, and soul ties.

√ I am free from fears, anxiety, stress, and worry.
√ I am free from all mental and emotional bondages, such as, depression, oppression, grief, guilt, and broken heartedness.
√ I am free from all unforgiveness, bitterness, resentment, hatred, self-unforgiveness, God unforgiveness, and unforgiveness for those living or dead.
√ I am free from all fatigue, tiredness, insomnia, and weariness.
√ I am free from all addictions (food, substance abuse) and destructive habits.
√ I am free from all sexual problems and impurities. I keep my mind pure.
√ I am free from all spirits of infirmity, sickness, and disease.
√ I am free from spirits of death and suicide.
√ I am free from all poverty, lack and debt. I loose prosperity, and all my bills are paid in Jesus' name.
√ I am free from all strongholds and bondages in my life
√ I am an overcomer in every area of my life. **[Rev 12:11]**
√ I am more than a conqueror through Jesus Christ. **[Romans 8:37]**
√ I boldly declare that I am free!

- ❖ Whom the Son sets free is free indeed! [**John 8:36**]

~Confession – My Ministry~

Speak this out of your mouth. Sow this in your heart and build it into your walk.

- ❖ Thank you Jesus, that according to [**2 Corinthians 5:17-20**], I am in Christ. I have been reconciled. You have given me a ministry of reconciliation. You have committed to me the Word of reconciliation.

- ❖ I have the motivation and ability to reconcile people back to you. I am Your ambassador.

- ❖ I thank you Father, that according to [**Luke 4:18-19**], Your Spirit is upon and in me.

- ❖ You have anointed me to preach the Gospel to the poor. You have sent me to heal the brokenhearted, to preach deliverance to the captives, recovery of sight to the blind, to set at liberty those that are bruised, oppressed, and broken down, to preach the acceptable year of the Lord, the day of salvation.

- ❖ In the name of Jesus, I boldly confess that I have received the Holy Spirit to be a witness to the Lord Jesus. I confess that I will go into all the world and I will preach the Gospel of salvation. [**Mark 16:15-20, Acts 1:8**]

- ❖ Thank You Lord, that I am as bold a lion. The righteous are as bold as a lion. I am righteous. [**Prov 28:1**]

- ❖ Thank You Father, that You have not given me a spirit of fear, but a spirit of power, love, and a sound mind. I am not a coward. In the name of Jesus I have boldness. I am more than a conqueror. I am engaged in God's military service. I am an enlisted person, and I endure hardness as a good soldier of the Lord Jesus Christ. [**2 Tim 2:3, 2 Tim 1:7, Rom 8:37**]

- ❖ I am motivated to fight for the will of God everywhere I am.

- Father, I am Your ambassador. If You are looking for someone to send, here I am, send me. [**Isaiah 6:8**]

- I will go for You. I am Your representative. I am a minister of reconciliation.

- I fully expect You to work with me to confirm Your Word that I speak out with signs following.

- I believe that we are co-laborers together. You are my strength and my results.

- I am Your mouthpiece. [**2 Cor 5:19-20, Mk 16:20, 2 Cor 3:9**] Speak to me; send me.

- The world awaits me, the lost await me. In the name of Jesus, I am wise because I win souls for the kingdom of God. Thank you Lord for making me an effective minister and witness for You. [**Prov 11:30**

NOTES

Chapter 24
Men Who Met God – Forefathers of Faith, Prayer and Revival

Raised With Him
By E.W. Kenyon

The Resurrection of the Lord Jesus is the proof of Satan's defeat, of man's Redemption, and of God's legal right to make the believer a New Creation.

[**Ephesians 1:7**] stands out with peculiar suggestiveness and comfort. "In whom we have our redemption through his blood, the remission of our trespasses, according to the riches of his grace." We have our Redemption. It is not something we have to pray or ask for. The moment we are Born Again, that moment Redemption is ours.

Satan's dominion over us ends. Our life of servitude and fear has come to an end. That Redemption is according to the riches of His grace. We are free.

[**Ephesians 2:6**], "And He raised us up with Him, and He made us to sit with Him in the heavenly places, in Christ Jesus." We were crucified with Him, died with Him, were buried with Him, suffered with Him, were justified with Him, were made alive with Him, conquered Satan with Him, and were raised together with Him.

That resurrection of Jesus is proof of our victory over the adversary. It is a proof that cannot be denied. Every person who takes Christ as Savior, in the mind of God, is a victor over the adversary.

So few of the Father's children have seen this mighty truth; that our victory was in the victory of Christ. When Jesus broke the bars of death, having conquered death, Satan, and sin, it was our victory.

[**Colossians 3:1**], "If then ye were raised together with Christ," and we were raised together with Christ. In the mind of the Father it was our translation out of the kingdom of darkness into the kingdom of the Son of His love. It was our Redemption. We had broken Satan's dominion over our body, soul, and spirit in Christ.

Walking in the Supernatural Power of Prayer

But perhaps the greatest message of our perfect victory over the adversary is found in [**Ephesians 1:19-22**]: "And what the exceeding greatness of his ability to us-ward who believe, according to that working of the strength of his might which he wrought in Christ, when he raised him from the dead, and made him to sit at his right hand in the heavenlies far above all rule, and authority, and power, and dominion, and every name that is named, not only in this age, but also in that which is to come: and he put all things in subjection under his feet, and gave him to be head over all things to the church, which is his body, the fullness of him that fills all in all."

The same ability that wrought in the dead body of Jesus to reanimate it and fill it with Immortality is today in the believer. We are today more than conquerors because of the life of God that was imparted to us in our New Creation.

It is the ability of God unveiled in that Resurrection that so shook the foundations of Hell, so that today, when the believers know that they were raised together with Christ, they know they are victors in every field and over every circumstance, and they may go on from triumph to triumph.

God has lifted the believer above all rule and authority and power and dominion, not only in this age, but in that which is to come. He put all things in subjection under the believer's feet. He gave Christ who is the head of the body to be master over all the forces of the universe.

Jesus gave to the believer a legal right to the use of His Name. He actually gave him the power of attorney so that in the Name of Jesus every demon and every power should obey that Name, in the lips of the believer.

There isn't anything too hard for God. God's ability is the ability that He gives to us, so His Resurrection is the proof of our right to reign over Satan and demons. He was raised because He had conquered Satan in our stead, so that we should no longer live in fear of the unseen forces of darkness.

The High Priest

In [**Matthew 28:6**] the angel said to the women who had come to finish the embalming of Jesus that Lord's Day morning: "Ye seek Jesus who was crucified, He is not here. He is risen. Come, see the place where the Lord lay." He died a Lamb. He arose the Lord High Priest of the New Creation.

Walking in the Supernatural Power of Prayer

You remember from [**John 20**] that Mary saw Him. When she discovered who He was, she fell at His feet. He said, "Touch me not; for I am not yet ascended unto the Father: but go unto my brethren, and say to them, I ascend unto my Father and your Father, and my God and your God." What did He mean?

He meant what we read in [**Hebrews 9:11-12**]: "But Christ having come a high priest of the good things to come, through the greater and more perfect tabernacle not made with hands, that is to say, not of this creation, nor yet with the blood of goats and calves, but with his own blood entered in once for all into the holy place, having obtained eternal redemption."

As the High Priest, He took His own blood and carried it up to the Heavenly Holy of Holies and there presented it to God. It was accepted, and that red seal is upon the document of our Redemption. The blood of Jesus Christ, God's Son, is the eternal witness of His finished work for us, of our legal right to Eternal Life, and sonship with all its privileges. On the basis of that blood, we are more than conquerors.

Satan has no dominion over us. His dominion is utterly broken. The tokens of that victory are continually before the Father.

[**Hebrews 7:22**], "By so much also hath Jesus become the surety of a better covenant." If you are in grave danger, or Satan is pressing hard upon you, you call the Father's attention to your rights that are guaranteed on the ground of that blood. [**Revelation 12:11**], "And they overcame him because of the blood of the Lamb, and because of the word of their testimony."

You have a legal right to the Name of Jesus that casts out demons and breaks Satan's power. [**John 16:23**], "If ye shall ask anything of the Father, he will give it you in my name." All things are possible to you, because you are in the family. You have the perfect protection that the blood guarantees.

Christ Sat Down

The climax of Redemption was the seating of the Lord Jesus. After He had been made sin, after He had paid the penalty of our relationship with Satan, after He had suffered all that Justice demanded of us, then Christ, with us, arose from the dead. We were raised with Him.

He declared we were seated together with Christ. [**Ephesians 2:6**], "And raised us up with him, and made us to sit with him in the heavenly places, in Christ Jesus." This was the highest honor that God had ever conferred upon man.

The Son became a man, identified Himself with the human race, delivered the human race from the authority of Satan, and carried His blood into the Holy of Holies to make the Eternal Redemption. Then He sat down at the right hand of the Majesty on High.

We have a man seated at God's right hand. He is our representative. He is there to represent us. This is the crowning event in Redemption, a man seated at God's right hand, and that man is the head of the new body, the Church. Is it any wonder he shouts, "Blessed be the God and Father of our Lord Jesus Christ, who hath blessed us with every spiritual blessing in the heavenly places in Christ"[**Ephesians 1:3**].

Not only are we seated in the highest position in the universe, but we are also blessed with every spiritual blessing that is necessary to maintain our place as members of His glorious body. In the mind of God, everyone of us is in Christ now. He sees us in Him.

When we go to the throne of Grace in prayer, it is as though Jesus were going there, for we go in His Name.

[**Colossians 3:3**], "For ye died, and your life is hid with Christ in God." We are hidden from the adversary, but we are visible to the Father.

[**Hebrews 9:24**], "For Christ entered not into a holy place made with hands, like in pattern to the true but into heaven itself, now to appear before the face of God for us." He is there at the right hand of the Father as our representative, as our Lord, as our Lover who gave Himself for us.

We can see that our redemption is a completed, finished thing. If Christ sat down at God's right hand, it is because the Father accepted Him and accepted what He did for us. The fact that He is seated there is the seal of our acceptance in the Beloved.

Joseph's Bones
by Charles Spurgeon
Proof of the power of Faith in laughing at improbabilities.

"And Joseph said to his brethren, I am dying; BUT GOD WILL SURELY VISIT YOU…and you shall carry up my bones from here…" [**Gen 50: 24,25**]

"By faith Joseph, when he was dying, made mention of the departure of the children of Israel, and gave instructions concerning his bones…" [**Heb 11:22**]

We cannot readily tell which action in a gracious life God may set the most store by. The Holy Spirit in this Chapter selects out of good men's lives the most brilliant instances of their Faith. I should hardly have expected that He would have mentioned the dying scene of Joseph's life as the most illustrious proof of his Faith in God. That eventful life— perhaps the most interesting in all Sacred Scripture, with the exception of One, abounds with incidents of which the Holy Spirit might have said by His servant Paul, *"By Faith Joseph did this and that,"* but none is mentioned save the closing scene. The triumph especially of his chastity under well-known and exceedingly severe temptation might have been very properly traced to the power of his Faith, but it is passed over, and the fact that he gave commandment concerning his bones is singled out as being the most illustrious proof of his Faith.

Joseph not only wished to be buried in Machpelah, which was natural, but he would not be buried there till the land was taken possession of… **he was so certain that they would come out of the captivity** that he postpones his burial till that glad event, and so makes what would have been but a natural wish, a means of expressing a **Holy and gracious confidence in the Divine Promise.**

He says, if you turn to the last Chapter of Genesis, *"I die, and **God will surely visit you"**;* or, as the text puts it, he *"made mention concerning the departing of the children of Israel."*…he bears his last witness to his brothers, who gather about his bed, concerning the **Faithfulness of God and the Infallibility of His Promise.**

Once more, here is a **proof of the power of Faith** in laughing at improbabilities.

If you will think of it, **it seemed a very unlikely thing that the children of Israel should go up out of Egypt; perhaps at the time when Joseph died, there appeared to be no reason why they should do so…**

But Joseph's eye was fixed upon the mighty Promise, *"In the fourth generation, they shall come here again"*; he knew that when the 400 years were passed, Abram's vision of the smoking furnace and the burning lamp would be fulfilled, and the Word would be established—*"And also that nation, whom they shall serve, will I judge: and afterward shall they come out with great substance."*

Though as yet he could not know that Moses would say, *"Thus says Jehovah, Let My people go"*; though he might not have foreseen the wonders at the Red Sea, and how Pharaoh and his chariots would be swallowed up there; and though he did not predict the wilderness, and the fiery cloudy pillar, and the heavens dropping manna, yet his Faith was firm that by some means the Covenant would be fulfilled!

Improbabilities were nothing to him, nor impossibilities either; **God has said it, and Joseph believes it!** On his dying bed, when fancy fades and strong delusion relaxes its iron grip, the true sure Faith of the man of God rose to its highest altitude, and like the evening star shed a sweet glory over the scene.
May we, my Beloved, possess the Faith which will triumph over all circumstances, and over every improbability that may apparently be connected with the Word of God!

In the case of Joseph, **his Faith led to an open avowal of his confidence in God's Promise.** On his deathbed he said, *"I die, but **God will visit you** and bring you up out of this land."* He also said, *"He will bring you to the land which He promised to Abraham, to Isaac, and to Jacob."*

Joseph, having thus declared his Faith, practically showed that he meant it, that it was not a matter of form, but a matter of heart! I do not know in what better way he could have shown his practical belief in the fact that God would bring the people out of Egypt than by saying, *"Keep my bones here; never bury them till you go yourselves to Canaan, having left Egypt forever, and taken possession of your Covenant country."*

He who believes in God will find practical ways of proving his Faith; he will avow it by an open confession….or if affliction is allotted to him by God, he will take it cheerfully, expecting that God will give him strength equal to the emergency, and so his Faith, by God's Grace, will triumph under the trial!

Moreover, notice that Joseph having Faith himself, he would encourage the Faith of others. No man may be said to have real Faith who is not concerned that Faith may be found in the hearts of his fellow men. *"But,"* you ask, *"What did Joseph do to encourage the Faith of others?"* Why, he left his bones to be a standing sermon to the children of Israel! Every time an Israelite thought of the bones of Joseph, he thought, *"We are to go out of this country one day."* He has left us the assurance of his confidence that God would in due time bring up His people out of this house of bondage."

Once more, it seems to me that Joseph's Faith in connection with his unburied bones showed itself in **his willingness to wait God's time for the Promised Blessing.** Says he, *"I believe I shall be buried in Machpelah, and I believe that my people will come up out of Egypt*; **I believe, and I am willing to wait**...**however weary may be the time of Israel's captivity! It is a great thing to have waiting Faith.** *"Stand still and see the salvation of God,"* is easier said than done….

Wait the Lord's appointment, O impatient Grumbler! Be quiet of spirit and calm of heart—**the vision will not tarry! Be willing to wait;** be willing to let your bones sleep in the dust till the trumpet of the Resurrection sounds, and if you could have a choice about it, refer your choice back again to your Lord in Heaven, for He knows what is best and right ….

You will notice that Joseph had his wish, for when Israel went up out of Egypt you will find, in the 15th of Exodus, that Moses took care to carry with them the bones of Joseph; and what is rather singular, those bones were not buried as soon as they came into Canaan; nor were they buried during the long wars of Joshua with the various tribes! But in the last verses of the book of Joshua, when nearly all the land had been conquered, and the country had been divided to the different tribes, and they had taken possession, then we read that they buried the bones of Joseph in the field of Shechem, in the place which Abraham had bought for a sepulcher. As if Joseph's remains might not be buried till they had won the country, until it was settled, and the Covenant was fulfilled. Then he must be buried, but not till then!

How blessed is waiting Faith which can let God take His time, and wait, believe in Him, let Him wait as long as He wills!

Though one after another we shall pass away, there are not dark days for our descendants, but **days of brightness are on the way.** *"Let Your work appear unto Your servants, and Your Glory unto their children."*
"He must reign till He has put all enemies under His feet." The kings of the isles shall yet acknowledge Him, and the wanderers of the desert shall bow down before Him! Jesus, the Christ of God, must be King over all the Earth, for God has sworn it, saying, *"Surely all flesh shall see the salvation of God."* **"The Glory of the Lord shall be revealed, and all flesh shall see it together: for the mouth of the Lord has spoken it."**

As Joseph said **"God will surely visit you"**

"Let us not grow weary while doing good, for in due season we shall reap if we do not lose heart" [**Galatians 6:9**]

Our Authority Over Sickness And The Devil – Gardner
By "The God of Miracles Lives Today" by Velmer Gardner – 1950

[**Mark 13:34**]: "For the Son of Man is as a man taking a far journey, who left his house, and gave authority to his servants, and to every man his work, and commanded the porter to watch." He gave **AUTHORITY** to his servants and to every man his work. Authority means the right to command obedience, the right to enforce obedience, and the right to act officially. Christ had authority over sickness and the devil. He had the right to command the sickness to leave and the devil had to obey. He had the right to enforce obedience, and He had the right to act in the official capacity as the Son of God.

The centurion came to Christ, and said, "My servant is sick at home and I want you to heal him." Jesus said, "I will go." The centurion said, "Jesus, you don't need to go and heal him, I am not worthy that you should enter under my roof, but speak the Word and my servant will be healed." He said, "I am a man of authority. The ones over me tell me what to do and I have to obey. I have authority over a hundred men. I will tell them to do this or do that and they do what I command them to do." And he said, "Now Christ, you have authority. You don't need to come to my home, all you have to do is say the Word and that sickness will have to leave because you have authority over it." And Jesus marveled and said, "I have not found such great faith, not in all Israel." (Paraphrased from [**Luke 7:3-9**].

The thing that brought healing to that centurion's servant was his faith in the authority there was in the Name of Jesus over sickness. And dear friend, today, if you have faith in the authority of the Name of Jesus over sickness you will be healed. The very moment that you appropriate that faith you will be healed. Healing comes as you recognize that Jesus has authority over sickness–all He has to do is speak the Word and it shall come to pass.

Now Christ gave His disciples this same authority. In [**Luke 9:1**] it says, "He called His twelve disciples together, and gave them power and authority over all devils, and to cure diseases." He said they were to preach the kingdom of God and to heal the sick. He gave them authority. Christ did not need this authority, He already had it. He gave this authority to His followers.

In [**Matthew 10:8**] Jesus told His disciples, "Heal the sick, cleanse the lepers, raise the dead, cast out devils: freely ye have received, freely give." Some people say we shouldn't preach on healing. Jesus preached and practiced healing. The disciples preached and practiced healing. The Word of God preaches healing, and I'm going to preach healing because God is a God of healing. He gave His disciples this authority. They went forth, and He went with them.

"Behold I give you authority over all the power of the enemy–over all the powers of the devil–over all the powers of hell–over every diabolical spirit or demon." [Paraphrased from **Matthew 10:1** and **Luke 9:1-2**]

Jesus has given that very same authority to us as His servants today. Christ has gone to heaven to prepare a glorious place for us, and what a place it must be. He has been there for nearly two thousand years getting it ready. He said, "I go to prepare a place for you. And if I go and prepare a place for you, I will come again, and receive you unto Myself; that where I am, there ye may be also," [**John 14:2-3**].

He is preparing a place where there will be no more sickness. There will be no more heartache. There will be no more funerals. There will be no more separations—no more poverty—no more weakness or tiredness. What a wonderful place! It will be reserved for the children of God. But listen, friends, while He is gone, He has not left His church down here to face the ravages of hell alone. Jesus said He was going to build His church upon a rock. It is going to take something to keep that church going while He is gone. He has given authority to His servants to carry on His work until He returns. He didn't give us the power to heal, but He gave us the **authority to use His power, "In His Name."**

There is not a businessman in America that would leave his business without someone in authority. He would have someone become the President of the firm while he was gone. He would have someone to be the custodian, someone to write the checks, someone to hire, and someone to take care of the bookkeeping. Every man would have his place, and that man would have authority over that certain position.

My dear friends, Jesus has gone away, and while He is gone He has given authority to His servants to carry on His work until He returns. I believe today, there are many people who are sick because they have not recognized the authority God has given His servants. They do not treat God's servants with the respect they are due.

Saul was a man that God blessed, anointed, and used in a tremendous way. Saul backslid, sinned, rejected God, and became a murderer and a terrible character. He even became demon possessed and died by suicide. The people told David to kill him, but David said, "Thou shalt not lay thine hands against God's anointed." [Paraphrased from **1 Samuel 24:6**]. David would not even lift his hand against this man that he had seen God use in such a tremendous way. He was afraid that the wrath of God might come upon him. So respect the servant of God. Respect your pastor, respect the evangelist, respect the missionaries, and respect the ones that have authority over you under God.

In [**James 5:14**] it says, "Is any sick among you? Let him call for the elders of the church; and let them pray over him, anointing him with oil in the name of the Lord." That friends, is exercising **POWER OF ATTORNEY**.

Christ has absolutely given us the legal right to use His name. He has given us authority to face the devil in the power of His name. He is not here, but He has given us authority to carry on His work until He comes. We can go forth using that power of attorney—using His name.

And my friends hear me now. **THE DEVIL HAS TO RECOGNIZE US WHEN WE USE THE POWER OF JESUS NAME,** just as though Jesus Christ Himself were standing before the devil and the devil would have to obey Him. We know that every time Jesus met the devil He defeated him. The devil was always defeated. Why? Because of the power and the authority Christ had. Christ has given us authority through the power of His name. Friends, He has not left us alone. He has given power and authority to His servants to carry on His work until He returns.

There is a difference between power and authority. No one has the power to heal, but we do have the power to exercise His authority. We have the authority to use His power. Then that power will bring healing—the Apostle Peter said, "In the Name of Jesus Christ of Nazareth rise up and walk," [**Acts 3:6**]. It was the first apostolic miracle performed. He recognized the authority there was in that Name, and he used that Name by faith. It did the work, and brother/sister, it will do it again today. There is power in the Name of Jesus, and we have authority to use that power, to use that Name. It's not the power of man. It's not the power of a church, but the power of Jesus' Name that brings healing today.

Now we have not the power to heal, but we have the authority to use His name. A policeman can stand down here at an intersection; a little hundred and twenty-five pound policeman. He holds out his hand, and the big logging truck stops. A big two hundred and twenty-five pound logger is in the truck. He says,

Walking in the Supernatural Power of Prayer

"Hurry up policeman, I'm in a rush." And the policeman says, "You'll go when I tell you to go." You'll never move until I tell you can move. Then the logger glares at him, and says to himself, "I could get out there and with one hand I could whip you. You haven't the power to stop me." It's true, he doesn't. The policeman knows he doesn't have the power, and the logger knows he doesn't have the power. But **THE POLICEMAN DOESN'T NEED THE POWER. He has been given the authority under the law to carry on and to fulfill the works of the law of the land**. And there is only one reason that logger stays there—he doesn't stay there because he's afraid of the power that this man has, because he knows the man hasn't the power to stop him. He knows that policeman has authority entrusted to him. If he violates that position of authority, and he runs past and resists the signals of that officer, he's going to have the whole city, the whole county, the whole state, and the whole United States after him. That policeman has been entrusted as an officer of the law and given authority to carry on the work of the law.

It is exactly the same thing in regard to God. God has not given any man the power to heal. There is not a man in the world who can heal anybody of anything, but God has given men the authority to use the power of Jesus' Name. Every man that God has called and ordained to preach the Gospel is a servant of God, and to that servant God has given authority to carry on His works until He returns. Every man will not have the same authority. Every man will not have the same talent-the same gift, but all of us have authority to carry on the works of Jesus until He returns. We can use the Name of Jesus with authority and it's going to produce works—it's going to produce the same works that Jesus produced when He was here. Jesus said, "The works that I do shall he do also; and greater works than these shall he do; because I go unto my Father," [**John 14:12**].

Oh, friends, the power is in the Name of Jesus. The devil trembles when he hears the Name of Jesus. We have authority to use that Name, to exercise it legally. Resist the devil. The devil has no claim upon a child of God. You can break every attack of the devil by the Name of Jesus. In the Name of Jesus, exercise the authority that God has given, and God will drive the devil's power back.

Jesus said, "I must work the works of Him that sent me, while it is day: the night cometh, when no man can work," [**John 9:4**]. In these dark closing days of time, as darkness is coming down upon the world, we must go forth and use the authority that God has given us. God has given us authority today over all the powers of sickness and over all the powers of the devil. When we pray for you, we demand in the

Walking in the Supernatural Power of Prayer

Name of Jesus that the devil release his hand from you. All sickness is the result of the devil. If there had never been a devil there would never have been any sickness.

Jesus has given us the authority to demand the devil to release his hand from you and the devil has to obey us. Friends, the devil has to obey us as His servants just as much as he would obey Jesus Christ. I say that reverently. I say that because I know it's the Word of God. In the Name of Jesus we can become bold. In the Name of Jesus we can make the devil fear us. There is power in the Name of Jesus, and we dare by faith to exercise that divine authority He has entrusted us with. All the power of hell has to flee. The powers of the enemy are defeated forever by the authority of Jesus Christ.

Every child of God has the legal right to use that name. Perhaps your child is epileptic. When one of those epileptic convulsions come upon it, God has given you power and authority to use that Name and command the epileptic demon of hell to leave that body and go back to hell where it belongs. It will have to obey you just as though Jesus Christ Himself were there because He is there. He's there in the power of His name. So when we pray for you friends, we exercise this authority. Through the Name of Jesus we come before the devil. We command the devil to release his power and the devil has to do it. God has not given us authority to heal, but He has given us authority to believe that He has already done it. You are already healed. Two thousand years ago Jesus healed every one of you just as much as He saved all of you. Believe Him now, and you'll be healed. Have faith in the authority of the name of Jesus like the centurion did. You don't have to beg and ask God for it, just believe Him. Take it by faith and stand upon God's Word, and God is going to honor it.

As servants of God, we are His ambassadors. An ambassador has no power, but he has authority to act in official capacities, and every nation recognizes the authority of an ambassador. If they don't treat that ambassador right, it won't be just the ambassador that they will have to contend with but the whole country, the whole government that is behind that ambassador. We are ambassadors of the King of Kings and Lord of Lords. We meet the devil and say, "Devil, take your hand off that body. Take your satanic influence away–take your oppressing hand from that body." And the devil says, "You haven't the power to make me do it. You haven't the power to cast me out." Sometimes the devil speaks forth boldly.

It's true, we tell the devil. We admit we don't have the power. We have no power. We are weak human beings with no power in ourselves, but we are not depending upon our power. We are ambassadors of the

Walking in the Supernatural Power of Prayer

Kingdom of Heaven. We have the authority to command that the devil obey us. We have the right to enforce the devil to obey us because God has given us authority in the Name of Jesus to demand the devil to do it. When we boldly take that stand, the devil is going to flee. He will flee from you. The Bible says so.

If the devil can bluff us and cause us to fear and tremble at his presence and power he will defeat us. But when we boldly meet the devil with, "Thus saith the Word of God," we claim our throne rights, and we claim our legal capacity in the Name of the Lord. When we say, "Devil, I stand as an ambassador of the kingdom of Heaven, and you are defeated in the Name of Jesus–I command you to listen to me–I command you to obey me–I command you to leave–I command you to take your hands from my body," then the healing power of Jesus will begin to flow because God recognizes that "power of attorney."

You exercise legal faith as you appropriate the power of Jesus Christ, and everything that Christ had or did is yours right then, through the power of His Name. Oh, let's believe Him friends. God has given authority to His servants, so let's have faith in God, and God will heal you. God wants to heal every one of you friends, and God will, if you will believe. So, when you are prayed for, have faith in this authority.

When you call for your pastor to pray for you and he lays hands on you, anoints you with oil, and prays the prayer of faith . . . right then friends, forget the man's hands. By faith, appropriate the nail scarred hands of Jesus–that's what it means: "And the prayer of faith shall save the sick, and the Lord shall raise him up," [**James 5:15**]. They can receive because they have come legally and claimed healing through the Name of Jesus.

Following Hard after God
by A. W. Tozer

My soul followeth hard after thee:
thy right hand upholdeth me. [**Psa. 63:8**]

Christian theology teaches the doctrine of prevenient grace, which briefly stated means this, that before a man can seek God, God must first have sought the man.

Before a sinful man can think a right thought of God, there must have been a work of enlightenment done within him; imperfect it may be, but a true work nonetheless, and the secret cause of all desiring and seeking and praying which may follow.

We pursue God because, and only because, He has first put an urge within us that spurs us to the pursuit. "No man can come to me," said our Lord, "except the Father which hath sent me draw him," and it is by this very prevenient drawing that God takes from us every vestige of credit for the act of coming. The impulse to pursue God originates with God, but the out working of that impulse is our following hard after Him; and all the time we are pursuing Him we are already in His hand: "Thy right hand upholdeth me."

In this divine "upholding" and human "following" there is no contradiction. All is of God, for as von Hugel teaches, God is always previous. In practice, however, (that is, where God's previous working meets man's present response) man must pursue God. Or, our part there must be positive reciprocation if this secret drawing of God is to eventuate in identifiable experience of the Divine. In the warm language of personal feeling this is stated in the Forty-second Psalm: "As the hart panteth after the water brooks, so panteth my soul after thee, O God. My soul thirsteth for God, for the living God: when shall I come. and appear before God?" This is deep calling unto deep, and the longing heart will understand it.

The doctrine of justification by faith-a Biblical truth, and a blessed relief from sterile legalism and unavailing self-effort has in our time fallen into evil company and been interpreted by many in such man ner as actually to bar men from the knowledge of God. The whole transaction of religious conversion has been made mechanical and spiritless. Faith may now be exercised without a jar to the moral life and without embarrassment to the Adamic ego. Christ may be "received" without creating any special love for Him in the soul of the receiver. The man is "saved," but he not hungry nor thirsty after God. In fact he is specifically taught to be satisfied and encouraged to be content with little.

The modern scientist has lost God amid the wonders of His world; we Christians are in real danger of losing God amid the wonders of His Word. We have almost forgotten that God is a Person and, as such, can be cultivated as any person can. It is inherent in personality to be able to know other personalities, but full knowledge of one personality by another cannot be achieved in one encounter. It is only after long and loving mental intercourse that the full possibilities of both can be explored.

All social intercourse between human beings is a response of personality to personality, grading upward from the most casual brush between man and man to the fullest, most intimate communion of which the human soul is capable. Religion, so far as it is genuine, is in essence the response of created personalities to the Creating Personality, God. "This is life eternal, that they might know thee the only true God, and Jesus Christ, whom thou hast sent."

God is a Person, and in the deep of His mighty nature He thinks, wills, enjoys, feels, loves, desires and suffers as any other person may. In making Himself known to us He stays by the familiar pattern of personality. He communicates with us through the avenues of our minds, our wills and our emotions. The continuous and unembarrassed interchange of love and thought between God and the soul of the redeemer man is the throbbing heart of New Testament religion.

This intercourse between God and the soul is known to us in conscious personal awareness. It is personal: that is, it does not come through the body of believers, as such, but is known to the individual, and, to the body through the individuals which compose it. And it is conscious: that is, it does not stay below the threshold of consciousness and work there unknown to the soul (as, for instance, infant baptism is though by some to do), but comes within the field of awareness where the man can "know" it as he knows any other fact of experience.

You and I are in little (our sins excepted) what, God is in large. Being made in His image we have: I within us the capacity to know Him. In our sins we lack only the power. The moment the Spirit has quickened us to life in regeneration our whole being senses its kinship to God and leaps up in joyous recognition That is the heavenly birth without which we cannon: see the Kingdom of God. It is, however, not an end but an inception, for now begins the glorious pursuit the heart's happy exploration of the infinite riches of the Godhead. That is where we begin, I say, but where: we stop no man has yet discovered, for there is in the awful and mysterious deaths of the Triune God neither limit nor end.

Shoreless Ocean, who can sound Thee?
Thine own eternity is round Thee,
    Majesty divine!

The Necessity of an Encounter
by A.W. Tozer

We are in tune with the plain teachings of the Bible when we attach *great importance* to genuine Christian *experience*. But I will take immediate objection to the charge, "Tozer preaches experience!"

I do not preach experience. I preach Christ. That is my calling, and I will always be faithful to that calling.

Nevertheless, I insist that the effective preaching of Jesus Christ, rightly understood, will *produce spiritual experience* in Christian believers. Moreover, if Christian preaching does *not* produce *spiritual experience* and *maturing* in the believer, the preaching is not being faithful to the Christ *revealed in the Scriptures!*

Let me say it again in another way. The Christ of the Bible is not rightly known until there is an *experience of Him within* the believer, for our Savior and Lord offers Himself to *human experience.*

Our shortcoming in spiritual experience is our tendency to believe without confirmation. God Himself does not need to confirm anything with His being. But we are not God. We are humans, and in matters of our faith we need confirmation within ourselves.

Why are so many Christian believers ineffective, anemic, disappointed, discouraged? I think the answer is that we need confirmation within ourselves, and we are not getting it.

I have no doubt that God, in love and grace and mercy, awaits to confirm His presence among those who will truly hunger and thirst after righteousness. For a long while I have been on record insisting that true spiritual experience is *conscious awareness* illustrated early in the Old Testament by Abram's personal realization and knowledge of *the presence of God.*

In the Christian Church, genuine spiritual experience goes back to the apostles---actually back to our Lord Himself. I do not refer to a dream while a person sleeps. I do not refer to something a person has buried in his or her subconsciousness. I refer to a *conscious intelligence, an awareness.*

The human personality has a right to be *consciously aware* of a meeting with God. There will be a spiritual confirmation, an *inward knowledge or witness.*

I repeat: Experience is *conscious awareness*. This kind of confirmation and witness was

Walking in the Supernatural Power of Prayer

taught and treasured by the great souls throughout the ages.

Conscious awareness of the presence of God! I defy any theologian or teacher to take that away from the believing church of Jesus Christ , But be assured they will try. And I refer not just to the liberal teachers. God has given us the Bible for a reason.

That reason is so it can *lead us to meet God in Jesus Christ in a clear, sharp encounter that will burn on in our hearts forever and ever!*

Genuine Christian experience must always include an *encounter with God Himself.* The spiritual giants of old were those who at so some time became acutely conscious of the presence of God maintained that consciousness for the rest of their lives.

The first encounter may have been one of terror, as when "an horror of great darkness" fell upon Abraham or as when Moses at the burning bush hid his face because he afraid to look upon God. But reading on, we learn that this fear soon lost its terror and changed rather to a delightful awe. Finally, it leveled off into a reverent sense of complete nearness to God. The essential point is this: These were men who met and experienced God!

Is it not that indeed they had become friends of God? Is it not that they walked in *conscious communion with the real Presence* and addressed their prayers to God with artless conviction that they were truly addressing Someone actually there?

The Spirit of God has compelled me to preach and write much about the believer's *conscious union with Christ* -- a union that must be *felt and experienced*. I will never be through talking about the union of the soul with the Savior, the conscious union of the believer's heart with Jesus. Remember, I am *not* talking about a theological union only. I am speaking also of a conscious union, a union that is felt and experienced.

For men and women who have met God, we may say that the sun -- the Son -- has come up in their hearts, and His warmth and light have given them a distinguishing radiance. They have the *inner witness.* Perhaps you will agree with me when I say, sadly, that *the average evangelical Christian is without this radiance.* Instead of a an inner witness, he or she too often is found substituting *logical conclusions drawn from Bible texts.* There is no witness, no encounter with God, no awareness of inner change. The whole point I am trying to make about the fellowship of a person with God is this: where there is a divine act within the s soul, there will be a *corresponding awareness*. This act of God is its own evidence. It addresses itself *directly to the spiritual consciousness.*

It is within this context of *awareness* and f*ellowship* and *communion* with God that I would comment on three abiding elements of Christian experience and spiritual life. These are elements that are a always the same among men and women who have had a personal meeting with God.

First, these great souls always have a *compelling sense of God Himself, of His person and of His presence.* While others would want to spend their time talking about a variety of things, these godly men and women, touched by their knowledge of God, want to talk about Him. They are drawn away from a variety of mundane topics because of the importance of their spiritual discoveries.

Second, it is plain that the *details and the significance* of their personal experiences remain *sharp and clear* with true spiritual meaning. I am not referring to any need or formula for identical Christian experiences. We ought to be fully aware that in the body of Christ we are not interested in the production of "cookie-cutter' Christians. God has given each of us an individual temperament and distinct characteristics. Therefore it is the office of the Holy Spirit to work out as He will the details in Christian experience. They will vary with personality.

Certainly, [though], we can be sure of this: whenever a person truly meets God in faith and commitment to the gospel, he will have a *consciousness* and a *sharp awareness* of the details of that spiritual transaction.

The third element is the *permanent and life changing nature of a true encounter with God.* The experience may have been brief, but the results will be evident in the life of the person touched as long a as he or she lives.

We can always trust the *moving and the leading of the Holy Spirit* in our lives and in our experiences. On the other hand, we ca cannot always trust our human leanings and our fleshly and carnal desires. That is why I am always a little suspicious of the *overly bubbly Christian* who talks too much about himself or herself and not enough about Jesus.

Then, I am always a little worried about the "hope-so" Christian who cannot tell me any of the details of his or her Christian experience.

And, I am more than a little concerned about the professing Christian whose experience does not seem to have resulted in a true *inner longing t*o be more like Jesus every day in thought, word and deed.

(Adapted from Chapter 1 of the book Men Who Met God, published by Christian Publications, Inc.)

Where Are the Elijahs of God to pray

by Leonard Ravenhill

The man who can get believers to praying would, under God, usher in the greatest revival that the world has ever known

To the question, "Where is the Lord God of Elijah?" we answer, "Where He has always been-on the throne!" But where are the Elijahs of God? We know Elijah was "a man of like passions as we are," but alas! we are not men of like prayer as he was. One praying man stands as a majority with God! Today God is bypassing men - not because they are too ignorant, but because they are too self-sufficient. Brethren, our abilities are our handicaps, and our talents our stumbling blocks!
Out of obscurity, Elijah came on to the Old Testament stage, a full-grown man. Queen Jezebel, that daughter of hell, had routed the priests of God and replaced them with groves to false deities. Darkness covered the land and gross darkness the people, and they were drinking iniquity like water. Every day the land, fouled with heathen temples and idolatrous rites, saw smoke curling from a thousand cruel altars.

All this was among a people who claimed Abraham as their father, and whose forebears had cried unto the Lord in their trouble and he had delivered them out of all their distresses. How the God of Glory had departed! the salt had lost its savour! the gold had become dim! But out of this measureless backsliding, God raised up a man-not a committee, not a sect, not an angel-but a MAN, and a man of like passions as we are! God *"sought for a man"* not to preach, but *"to stand in the gap."*

As Abraham, so now Elijah *"stood before the Lord"* Therefore the blessed Holy Spirit could right the life of Elijah in two words: *"He prayed"* No man can do more than that for God or for men. If the Church today had as many agonizers as she has advisers, we would have a revival in a year!

Such praying men are always our national benefactors. Elijah was such. He had heard a voice, seen a vision, tasted a power, measured an enemy, and, with God as partner, wrought a victory. The tears he shed, the soul agonies he endured, the groans he uttered, are all recorded in the book of the chronicles of the things of God. A last Elijah emerged to prophecy with divine infallibility. He knew the mind of God. Therefore he-one man- strangled a nation and altered the course of nature. This "crag of a man" stood as majestic and immovable as the mountains of Gilead, as he shut up the heavens with a word. Though it is wonderful indeed when God lays hold of a man, earth can know one greater wonder-when a man lays hold of God. Let a man of God "in the Spirit" *groan,* and God will cry out *"Let Me alone."* We would like Elijah's accomplishments, but not His banishments!

Brethren, if we will do God's work in God's way, at God's time, with God's power, we shall have God's blessing and the devil's curses. When God opens the windows of heaven to bless us, the devil will open the doors of hell to blast us. God's smile means the devil's frown! Mere preachers may help anybody and hurt nobody; but prophets will stir everybody and madden somebody. The preacher may go with the crowd; the prophet goes against it. A man freed, fired, and filled with God will be branded unpatriotic because he speaks against his nation's sins; unkind because his tongue is a two-edged sword; unbalanced because the weight of preaching opinion is against him. Preachers make pulpits famous; prophets make prisons famous. The preacher will be heralded; the prophet hounded.

Ah! brother preachers, we love the old saints, missionaries, martyrs, reformers: our Luthers, Bunyans, Wesleys, Asburys, etc. We will write their biographies, reverence their memories, frame their epitaphs, and build their monuments. We will do anything except imitate them. We cherish the last drop of their blood, but watch carefully the first drop of our own!

John the Baptist did well to evade prison for six months. He and Elijah would not last six weeks in the streets of a modern city. They would be cast into prison or mental home for judging sin and not muting their message.
Elijah lived with God. He thought about the nation's sin like God; he grieved over sin like God; he spoke against sin like God. He was all passion in his prayers and passionate in his denunciation of evil in the land. He had no smooth preaching. Passion fired his preaching, and his words were on the hearts of men as molten metal on their flesh.

But *"The steps of a good man are ordered by the Lord"* [**Psalm 37:23**]. The Lord said to Elijah, *"Hide thyself,"* and again, *"Show thyself."* It would be wrong to hide when we should be rebuking kings for His sake; it would be wrong to preach if the Spirit is calling us to wait upon the Lord. We must learn with David, *"My soul wait thou only upon God"* [**Psalm 62:5**]

Who of is dares to invite the Lord to cut out all our props? God's ways are not our ways. His ways are *" past finding out,"* but HE REVEALS THEM TO US BY HIS SPIRIT!

Elijah prayed, not for the destruction of the idolatrous priests, nor for thunderbolts from heaven to consume rebellious Israel, but that the GLORY OF GOD and the POWER OF GOD MIGHT BE REVEALED!

We try to help God out of difficulties. Remember how Abraham tried to do this, and to this day the earth is cursed with his folly because of Ishmael. On the other hand, Elijah made it as difficult as he could for the Lord. He wanted fire, but yet he soaked the sacrifice with water! God loves such holy boldness in our prayers. *"Ask of Me, and I shall give thee the heathen for thine inheritance, and the uttermost parts of the earth for thy possession."* [**Psalm 2:8**]

Oh, my ministering brethren! Much of our praying is but giving God advice. Our praying is discolored with ambition, either for ourselves or for our denomination. Perish the thought! Our goal must be God alone. It is His honor that is defiled, His blessed Son who is ignored, His laws broken, His name profaned, His book forgotten, His house made a circus of social efforts.
Does God ever need more patience with His people than when they are "praying"? We tell Him what to do and then how to do it. We pass judgments and make appreciations in our prayers. In short, we do everything except pray! No Bible school can teach us this art. What Bible school has "prayer" on its curriculum? The most important thing a man can study is the prayer part of the book. But where is this taught? Let us strip off the last bandage and declare that many of our presidents and teachers do not pray, shed no tears, know no travail. Can they teach what they do not know?

The man who can get believers to praying would, under God, usher in the greatest revival that the world has ever known. There is no fault in God. He is able. God *"is able to do according to the power that worketh in us."* God's problem today is not communism, nor yet Romanism, nor liberalism, nor modernism. God's problem is - dead fundamentalism!

This generation of preachers is responsible for this generation of sinners. At the very doors of our churches are the masses - unwon because they are unreached, unreached because they are unloved. Thank God for all that is being done for missions overseas. Yet it is strangely true that we can get more "apparent" concern for people across the world than for our perishing neighbors across the street! With all our mass-evangelism, souls are won only in hundreds. Let an atom bomb come and they will fall by the millions into hell.

Sin today is both glamorized and popularized, thrown into the ear by radio, thrown into the eye by television, and splashed on popular magazine covers. Churchgoers, sermon-sick and teaching-tired, leave the meeting as they entered it - visionless and passionless! Oh God, give this perishing generation ten thousand John the Baptists!

Just as Moses could not mistake the sight of the burning bush, so a nation could not mistake the sight of a burning man! God meets fire with fire. John the Baptist was a new man with a new message. As a man accused of murder hears the dread cry of the judge, "Guilty!" and pales at it, so the crowd heard John's cry, "Repent!" until it rang down the corridors of their minds, stirred memory, bowed the conscience and brought them terror-stricken to repentance and baptism! After Pentecost, the onslaught of Peter, fresh from his fiery baptism of the Spirit, shook the crowd until as one man they cried out: "Men and brethren, what shall we do?" Imagine someone telling these sin-stricken men, "Just sign a card! Attend church regularly! Pay your tithes!" No! A thousand times no!

Questions:

1. Is it possible to have passion without prayer?

2. What must we be willing to give up in order to obtain the mind of Christ?

3. Would you prefer God to have partnership with you or to have ownership of you?

4. What can you do to stimulate prayer in your local church and in corporate multi-church prayer meetings?

From *Why Revival Tarries* by Leonard Ravenhill,

Walking in the Supernatural Power of Prayer

√ Lets unleash the power of prayer on our adversary by putting prayer back in first place as we partner with Jesus in "destroying the works of the evil one." H. A. Lewis

When I was 9, I started boxing which was short lived one. I ended up to have a total of 102 fights in the ring, losing none. I was five foot three and a whopping 105 lbs. Not exactly a physical specimen. But I wanted to learn to fight and I reasoned that even if I never became a champion I could learn some things that would help me protect myself.

I was taught to be a tough guy and was known all around the city. In many ways over the years I counted it as survival in my life. I was taught to not back down from your opponent and be a warrior. Grow strength of good character and be a defender of the weak. I didn't know it back then but God in his infinite wisdom was not missing out on a chance to train me. What looked like a failure to me was the beginning of my spiritual warfare school.

[1 Peter 5:8] *Be alert and of sober mind. Your enemy the devil prowls around like a roaring lion looking for someone to devour.*

It has been helpful to me over the years to recognize that life is a battle and like it or not we have all been placed in the ring with an opponent that is carrying out an attack against us and he never takes a break. There is only one way to win a boxing match and that is to go on the offense. A good defense is important but if all you do is block punches you will never win.

Imagine the insanity of a boxer stepping into a ring and never throwing punches yet this is often the posture we have as believers. We are so busy blocking punches we are not throwing any back. Like me when I saw the kid with the facial hair I was defeated before I even started. I took it a step further and gave up altogether.

In boxing your posture is important. You learn right away how to stand in such a way to be a more difficult target. To hold your shoulder or elbow in the just the right place to protect yourself more. How to move from side to side, and lunge forward when necessary. But all this moving , posturing, and protecting is unto one thing. Landing punches of your own.

On the offensive side of things you learn that the "jab" is meant to keep the opponent busy and keep him off balance so you can set him up for the power punch. You are always looking to land that knock out blow.

There are many ways we can go on the offense but prayer is the primary weapon in the arsenal. It can be done from anywhere and at any time. It can be done alone or with others. From one location you can have influence across the earth.

Watchman Nee the great apostle of China had this to say about prayer:
"Prayer is work. The experiences of many children of God demonstrate that it accomplishes far more than does any other form of work. It is also warfare, for it is one of the weapons in fighting the enemy."

E. M. Bounds had this to say when expounding on Paul the apostle's teachings:
"His teaching is that praying is the most important of all things on earth. All else must be restrained and retired to give it primacy. Put it first and keep it's primacy. The conflict is about the primacy of prayer. Defeat and victory lie in this one thing. To make prayer secondary is to dis-crown it. It is to fetter and destroy prayer. If prayer is put first then God is put first, and victory is assured."

When we pray we are going on the offensive. When we pray with persistence we are jabbing, jabbing, jabbing, and making the enemy's job very difficult. When we pray the scriptures we destroy the lies of the enemy with the truth of God. When we pray all the way through to victory we deliver the knockout blow we are looking for.

Ten Characteristics of Revival in the Scripture
by Dr. Bob Griffin

<u>Twelve Revivals in the Old Testament</u>—Jacob: [**Gen 35:1-15; Asa: 2 Chr 15:1-15; Jehoash: 2 Kgs 11-12/2 Chr 23-24; Hezekiah: 2 Kgs 18:4-7/2 Chr 29-31; Josiah: 2 Kgs 22-23; Ezra: Ez 5-6; Nehemiah/Ezra: Neh 8:9/12:44-47; Jonah; Jehoshaphat: 2 Chr 17:6-9, & Chp. 20; Moses: Exod 32-33; Samuel: I Sam 7:1-13; Elijah: I Kgs 18**]

<u>Eight Revivals in the New Testament</u>—John the Baptist:[**Matt 3:1-12; Pentecost: Acts 2:1-4, 14-47**; the Church: **Acts 4:23-37**; Ananias and Sapphira: **Acts 5:1-16**; Stephen's sermon and death: **Acts 7:54-8:25**; Cornelius: **Acts 10: 23-48**; Pisidian Antioch: **Acts 13:44-52; Ephesus: Acts 19:1-20**

Confirmed in History:

Through the First and Second Great Awakenings--1726 and 1776, the New York City Prayer Meeting Revival--1857, the Azusa Street Revival--1906 and the Welsh Revival of 1904.

1. Revival occurred in a time of deep moral darkness and national depression, personal or national crisis, a time of spiritual decline or apostasy among God's people Israel or his Church and generally a time of great spiritual need.

2. Revival began in the heart of one or more consecrated servants of God, who became the energizing power behind the revival, the agent or agents used of God to lead God's people back to faith in God and obedience to him.

3. Prayer was central to revival. Leaders called out to God in prayer and in many instances, led God's people to do the same, passionately seeking God's face in repentance and in the confession of their personal and national sins.

4. Revival rested upon the powerful teaching, proclamation or preaching of the Word or law of God, and many of the revivals were the result of a return to the Law or Word.

5. Revival in the Old Testament was dominated by God the Father for the awakening of his people Israel to a restored relationship with him, to obedience and to serving his purposes. Revival in the New Testament was dominated by the work of the Holy Spirit and miracles for the equipping of people for ministry, and it resulted in the spread of the gospel and the growth of the Church.

6. Revival was marked by a return to the worship of God.

7. Revival witnessed a destruction of idols or ungodly preoccupations, a separation from personal and corporate sin.

8. Revival witnessed a return to the offering of blood sacrifices in the Old Testament and a

concentration on the death, resurrection and return of Jesus Christ in the New Testament, celebrated in the Lord's Supper.

9. Revival resulted in an experience of exuberant joy and gladness among the people of God.

10. Revival was followed by a period of blessing and/or social reform.

Definition Of Revival

+"Revival is a spontaneous spiritual awakening by God the Holy Spirit among God's people.

+ It results from their humble prayers,
+ when they passionately seek God's face, and
+ repent for their sins.
+ The awakening results in deepened intimacy with God, passion for Him, holy living,

Walking in the Supernatural Power of Prayer

In Word, Or In Power
by A.W. Tozer

Excerpted from The Divine Conquest

For our gospel did not come to you in word only, but also in power, and in the Holy Spirit and with deep conviction, as you know what kind of men we were among you for your sake.
[1 Ths. *1:5*]

If anyone is in Christ, he is a new creation. [2 Cor. 5:17]
You have a reputation of being alive, but you are dead. [Rev. 3:1]

To one who is a student merely, these verses might be interesting, but to a serious man intent upon gaining eternal life they might well prove more than a little disturbing. For they evidently teach that the message of the gospel may be received in either of two ways: in word only, without power, or in word with power. Yet it is the same message whether it comes in word or in power. And these verses teach also that when the message is received in power it effects a change so radical as to be called a new creation. But the message may be received without power, and apparently some have so received it, for they have a name to live, and are dead. All this is present in these texts.

By observing the ways of men at play I have been able to understand better the ways of men at prayer. Most men, indeed, play at religion as they play at games, religion itself being of all games the one most universally played. The various sports have their rules and their balls and their players; the game excites interest, gives pleasure, and consumes time, and when it is over, the competing teams laugh and leave the field. It is common to see a player leave one team and join another and a few days later play against his old mates with as great zest as he formerly displayed when playing *for* them. The whole thing is arbitrary. It consists in solving artificial problems and attacking difficulties that have been deliberately created for the sake of the game. It has no moral roots and is not suppose d to have. No one is the better for his self-imposed toil. It is all but a pleasant activity that changes nothing and settles nothing at last.

If the conditions we describe were confined to the ballpark, we might pass it over without further thought, but what are we to say when this same spirit enters the sanctuary and decides the attitude of men toward God and religion? For the Church has also its fields and its rules and its equipment for playing the game of pious words. It has its devotees, both laymen and professionals, who support the game with their money and encourage it with their presence, but who are no different in life or character from many who take in religion no interest at all.

As an athlete uses a ball, so do many of us use words: words spoken and words sung, words written and words uttered in prayer. We throw them swiftly across the field; we learn to handle them with dexterity and grace; we build reputations upon our word skill and gain as our reward the applause of those who have enjoyed the game. But the emptiness of it is apparent from the fact that after the pleasant religious game *no one is basically any different from what he had been before.* The basis of life remains unchanged; the same old principles govern, the same old Adam rules.

I have not said that religion without power makes no changes in a man's life, only that it makes no fundamental difference. Water may change from liquid to vapor, from vapor to snow, and back to liquid again, and still be fundamentally the same. So powerless religion may put a man through many surface changes and leave him exactly what he was before. Right there is where the snare lies. *The changes are in form only; they are not in kind.* Behind the activities of the nonreligious man and the man who has received the gospel without power lie the very same motives. An unblessed ego lies at the bottom of both lives, the difference being that the religious man has learned better to disguise his vice. His sins are refined and less offensive than before he took up religion, but the man himself is no t a better man in the sight of God. He may indeed be a worse one, for always God hates artificiality and pretense. Selfishness still throbs like an engine at the center of the man's life. True he may learn to "redirect" his selfish impulses, but his woe is that self still lives unrebuked and even unsuspected deep within his heart. He is a victim of religion without power.

The man who has received the Word without power has trimmed his hedge, but it is a thorn hedge still and can never bring forth the fruits of the new life. Men do not gather grapes from thorns nor figs from thistles. Yet such a man may be a leader in the church, and his influence and his vote may go far to determine what religion shall be in his generation.

Walking in the Supernatural Power of Prayer

The Old Adam to the New Adam - H.A.Lewis

The truth received in power shifts the basis of life from Adam to Christ, and a new set of motives goes to work within the soul.

A new and different Spirit enters the personality and makes the believing man new in every department of his being. His interests shift from things external to things internal, from things on earth to things in heaven. He loses faith in the soundness of external values, he sees clearly the deceptiveness of outward appearances, and his love for and confidence in the unseen and eternal world become stronger as his experience widens.

With the ideas here expressed most Christians will agree, but the gulf between theory and practice is so great as to be terrifying. For the gospel is too often preached and accepted without power, and the radical shift that the truth demands is never made. There may be, it is true, a change of some kind; an intellectual and emotional bargain may be struck with the truth, but whatever happens is not enough, not deep enough, not radical enough. The "creature" is changed, but he is not "new." And right there is the tragedy of it. The gospel is concerned with a new life, with a birth upward onto a new level of being, and until it has effected such a rebirth it has not done a saving work within the soul.

Wherever the Word comes without power its essential content is missed. For there is in divine truth an imperious note; there is about the gospel an urgency, a finality that will not be heard or felt except by the enabling of the Spirit. We must constantly keep in mind that the gospel is not good news only, but a judgment as well upon everyone that hears it. The message of the Cross is good news indeed for the penitent, but to those who "obey not the gospel" it carries an overtone of warning. The Spirit's ministry to the impenitent world is to tell of sin and righteousness and judgment. For sinners who want to cease being willful sinners and become obedient children of God, the gospel message is one of unqualified peace, but it is by its very nature also an arbiter of the future destinies of men.

This secondary aspect is almost wholly overlooked in our day. The *gift* element in the gospel is held to be its exclusive content, and the *shift* element is accordingly ignored. Theological assent is all that is required to make Christians. This assent is called faith and is thought to be the only difference between the saved and the lost. Faith is thus conceived as a kind of religious magic, bringing to the Lord great delight and possessing mysterious power to open the Kingdom of heaven.

I want to be fair to everyone and to find all the good I can in every man's religious beliefs, but the harmful effects of this faith-as-magic creed are greater than could be imagined by anyone who has not come face-to-face with them. Large assemblies today are being told fervently that the one essential qualification for heaven is to be an evil man, and the one sure bar to God's favor is to be a good one. The very word *righteousness* is spoken only in cold scorn, and the moral man is looked upon with pity. "A Christian," say these teachers, "is not morally better than a sinner; the only difference is that he has taken Jesus, and so he has a Savior." I trust it may not sound flippant to inquire, *"A savior from what?"* If not from sin and evil conduct and the old fallen life, then from what? And if the answer is, "From the consequences of past sins and from judgment to come," still we are not satisfied. Is justification from past offenses all that distinguishes a Christian from a sinner? Can a man become a believer in Christ and be no better than he was before? Does the gospel offer no more than a skillful Advocate to get guilty sinners off free at the Day of Judgment?

I think the truth of the matter is not too deep nor too difficult to discover. Self-righteousness is an effective bar to God's favor because it throws the sinner back upon his own merits and shuts him out from the imputed righteousness of Christ. And to be a sinner confessed and consciously lost *is* necessary to the act of receiving salvation through our Lord Jesus Christ. This we joyously admit and constantly assert, but here is the truth that has been overlooked in our day: *A sinner cannot enter the Kingdom of God.*

The Bible passages that declare this are too many and too familiar to need repeating here, but the skeptical might look at [**Galatians 5:19-21**] and [**Revelation 21:8**]. How then can any man be saved? The penitent sinner meets Christ, and after that saving encounter he is a sinner no more. The power of the gospel changes him, shifts the basis of his life from self to Christ, faces him about in a new direction, and makes him a new creation.

The moral state of the penitent when he comes to Christ does not affect the result, for the work of Christ sweeps away both his good and his evil, and turns him into another man. The returning sinner is not saved by some judicial transaction apart from a corresponding moral change. Salvation must include a judicial change of status, but what is overlooked by most teachers is that *it also includes an actual change in the life of the individual.* And by this we mean more than a surface change; we mean a transformation as deep as the roots of his human life. If it does not go that deep, it does not go deep enough.

If we had not first suffered a serious decline in our expectations, we should not have accepted this tame technical view of faith. The churches (even the gospel churches) are worldly in spirit, morally anemic, on the defensive, imitating instead of initiating, and in a wretched state generally because for two full generations they have been told that justification is no more than a not guilty verdict pronounced by the heavenly Father upon a sinner who can present the magic in *faith* with the wondrous "open sesame" engraved upon it. If it is not stated as bluntly as that, at least the message is so presented as to create such an impression. The whole business is the result of hearing the Word preached without power and receiving it in the same way.

Now faith is indeed the open sesame to eternal blessedness. Without faith it is impossible to please God; neither can any man be saved apart from faith in the risen Savior. But the true quality of faith is almost universally missed, namely, its moral quality. It is more than mere confidence in the veracity of a statement made in Holy Writ. It is a highly moral thing and of a spiritual essence. It invariably effects radical transformation in the life of the one who exercises it. It shifts the inward gaze from self to God. It introduces its possessor into the life of heaven upon earth.

It is not my desire to minimize the justifying effect of faith. No man who knows the depths of his own wickedness would dare to appear before the ineffable Presence with nothing to recommend him but his own character, nor would any Christian, wise after the discipline of failures and imperfections, want his acceptance with God to depend upon any degree of holiness to which he might have attained through the operations of inward grace. All who know their own hearts and the provisions of the gospel will join in the prayer of the man of God:

Walking in the Supernatural Power of Prayer

When He shall come with trumpet sound,
O may I then in Him be found;
Dressed in His righteousness alone,
Faultless to stand before the throne.

It is a distressing thing that a truth so beautiful should have been so perverted. But perversion is the price we pay for failure to emphasize the moral content of truth; it is the curse that follows rational orthodoxy when it has quenched or rejected the Spirit of Truth.

In asserting that faith in the gospel effects a change of life motive from self to God, I am but stating the sober facts. Every man with moral intelligence must be aware of the curse that afflicts him inwardly; he must be conscious of the thing we call ego, by the Bible called flesh or self, but by whatever name called, a cruel master and a deadly foe. Pharaoh never ruled Israel as tyrannically as this hidden enemy rules the sons and daughters of men.

The words of God to Moses concerning Israel in bondage may well describe us all: "I have indeed seen the misery of My people in Egypt. I have heard them crying out because of their slave drivers, and I am concerned about their suffering." And when, as the Nicene Creed so tenderly states, our Lord Jesus Christ, "for us men, and for our salvation came d own from heaven, and was incarnate by the Holy Spirit of the Virgin Mary, and was made man, and was crucified also for us under Pontius Pilate, and suffered and was buried, and the third day He arose again according to the Scriptures, and ascended into heaven, and sits at the right hand of the Father," what was it all for? That He might pronounce us technically free and leave us in our bondage? Never. Did not God say to Moses, "I have come down to rescue them from the hand of the Egyptians and to bring them up out of that land into a good and spacious land, a land flowing with milk and honey"? For sin's human captives God never intends anything less than full deliverance. The Christian message rightly understood means this: The God, who by the *word* of the gospel *proclaims* men free, by the *power* of the gospel *actually makes them free.* To accept less than this is to know the gospel in word only, without its power.

They to whom the Word comes in power know this deliverance, this inward migration of the soul from slavery to freedom, this release from moral bondage. They know in experience a radical shift in position, a real crossing over, and they stand consciously on another soil under another sky and breath another air. Their life motives are changed and their inward drives made new.

What are these old drives that once forced obedience at the end of a lash? What but little taskmasters, servants of the great taskmaster *Self*, who stand before him and do his will? To name them all would require a book in itself, but we would point out one as a type of sample of the rest. It is the desire for social approval. This is not bad in itself and might be perfectly innocent if we were living in a sinless world, but since the race of men has fallen off from God and joined itself to His foes, to be a friend of the world is to be a collaborator with evil and an enemy of God. Still the desire to please men is back of all social acts from the highest civilizations to the lowest levels upon which human life is found. No one can escape it. The outlaw who flouts the rules of society and the philosopher who rises in thought above its common ways may *seem* to have escaped from the snare, but they have in reality merely narrowed the circle of those they desire to please. The outlaw has his pals before whom he seeks to shine; the philosopher his little coterie of superior thinkers whose approval is necessary to his happiness. For both, the motive root remains uncut. Each draws his peace from the thought that he enjoys the esteem of his fellows, though each will interpret the whole business in his own way.

Every man looks to his fellowmen because he has no one else to whom he can look. David could say, "Whom have I in heaven but You? And earth has nothing I desire besides You," but the sons of this world have not God; they have only each other, and they walk holding to each other and looking to one another for assurance like frightened children. But their hope will fail them, for they are like a group of men, none of whom has learned to fly a plane, who suddenly find themselves aloft without a pilot, each looking to the other to bring them safely down. Their desperate but mistaken trust cannot save them from the crash which must certainly follow.

With this desire to please men so deeply implanted within us, how can we uproot it and shift our life drive from pleasing men to pleasing God? Well, no one can do it alone; nor can he do it with the help of others, nor by education, nor by training, nor by any other method known under the sun. What is required is a reversal of nature (that it is a fallen nature does not make it any the less powerful), and this reversal must be a supernatural act. That act the Spirit performs through the power of the gospel when it is received in living faith. Then He displaces the old with the new. Then He invades the life as sunlight invades a landscape and drives out the old motives as light drives away darkness from the sky.

The way it works in experience is something like this: The believing man is overwhelmed suddenly by a powerful feeling that *only God matters*; soon this works itself out into his mental life and conditions all his judgments and all his values. Now he finds himself free from slavery to man's opinions. A mighty desire to please only God lays hold of him. Soon he learns to love above all else the assurance that he is well pleasing to the Father in heaven.

It is this complete switch in their pleasure source that has made believing men invincible. So could saints and martyrs stand alone, deserted by every earthly friend, and die for Christ under the universal displeasure of mankind. When, to intimidate him, Athanasius' judges warned him that the whole world was against him, he dared to reply, "Then is Athanasius against the world!" That cry has come down the years and today may remind us that the gospel has power to deliver men from the tyranny of social approval and make them free to do the will of God.

I have singled out this one enemy for consideration, but it is only one, and there are many others. They seem to stand by themselves and have existence apart from each other, but it is only seeming. Actually they are but branches of the same poison vine, growing from the same evil root, and they die together when the root dies. That root is *self*, and the Cross is its only effective destroyer.

The message of the gospel, then, is the message of a new creation in the midst of an old, the message of the invasion of our human nature by the eternal life of God and the displacing of the old by the new. The new life seizes upon the believing man's nature and sets about its benign conquest, a conquest that is not complete until the invading life has taken full possession and a new creation has emerged. And this is an act of God without human aid, for it is a moral miracle and a spiritual resurrection.

Walking in the Supernatural Power of Prayer

The Old Cross and the New
by A.W.Tozer

ALL UNANNOUNCED AND MOSTLY UNDETECTED there has come in modern times a new cross into popular evangelical circles. It is like the old cross, but different: the likenesses are superficial; the differences, fundamental.

From this new cross has sprung a new philosophy of the Christian life, and from that new philosophy has come a new evangelical technique-a new type of meeting and a new kind of preaching. This new evangelism employs the same language as the old, but its content is not the same and its emphasis not as before.

The old cross would have no truck with the world. For Adam's proud flesh it meant the end of the journey. It carried into effect the sentence imposed by the law of Sinai. The new cross is not opposed to the human race; rather, it is a friendly pal and, if understood aright, it is the source of oceans of good clean fun and innocent enjoyment. It lets Adam live without interference. His life motivation is unchanged; he still lives for his own pleasure, only now he takes delight in singing choruses and watching religious movies instead of singing bawdy songs and drinking hard liquor. The accent is still on enjoyment, though the fun is now on a higher plane morally if not intellectually.

The new cross encourages a new and entirely different evangelistic approach. The evangelist does not demand abnegation of the old life before a new life can be received. He preaches not contrasts but similarities. He seeks to key into public interest by showing that Christianity makes no unpleasant demands; rather, it offers the same thing the world does, only on a higher level. Whatever the sin-mad world happens to be clamoring after at the moment is cleverly shown to be the very thing the gospel offers, only the religious product is better.

The new cross does not slay the sinner, it redirects him. It gears him into a cleaner and jollier way of living and saves his self-respect. To the self-assertive it says, "Come and assert yourself for Christ." To the egotist it says, "Come and do your boasting in the Lord." To the thrill seeker it says, "Come and enjoy the thrill of Christian fellowship." The Christian message is slanted in the direction of the current vogue in order to make it acceptable to the public.

The philosophy back of this kind of thing may be sincere but its sincerity does not save it from being false. It is false because it is blind. It misses completely the whole meaning of the cross.

The old cross is a symbol of death. It stands for the abrupt, violent end of a human being. The man in Roman times who took up his cross and started down the road had already said good-by to his friends. He was not coming back. He was going out to have it ended. The cross made no compromise, modified nothing, spared nothing; it slew all of the man, completely and for good. It did not try to keep on good terms with its victim. It struck cruel and hard, and when it had finished its work, the man was no more.

The race of Adam is under death sentence. There is no commutation and no escape. God cannot approve any of the fruits of sin, however innocent they may appear or beautiful to the eyes of men. God salvages the individual by liquidating him and then raising him again to newness of life.

Walking in the Supernatural Power of Prayer

That evangelism which draws friendly parallels between the ways of God and the ways of men is false to the Bible and cruel to the souls of its hearers. The faith of Christ does not parallel the world, it intersects it. In coming to Christ we do not bring our old life up onto a higher plane; we leave it at the cross. The corn of wheat must fall into the ground and die.

We who preach the gospel must not think of ourselves as public relations agents sent to establish good will between Christ and the world. We must not imagine ourselves commissioned to make Christ acceptable to big business, the press, the world of sports or modern education. We are not diplomats but prophets, and our message is not a compromise but an ultimatum.

God offers life, but not an improved old life. The life He offers is life out of death. It stands always on the far side of the cross. Whoever would possess it must pass under the rod. He must repudiate himself and concur in God's just sentence against him.

What does this mean to the individual, the condemned man who would find life in Christ Jesus? How can this theology be translated into life? Simply, he must repent and believe. He must forsake his sins and then go on to forsake himself. Let him cover nothing, defend nothing, excuse nothing. Let him not seek to make terms with God, but let him bow his head before the stroke of God's stern displeasure and acknowledge himself worthy to die.

Having done this let him gaze with simple trust upon the risen Saviour, and from Him will come life and rebirth and cleansing and power. The cross that ended the earthly life of Jesus now puts an end to the sinner; and the power that raised Christ from the dead now raises him to a new life along with Christ.

To any who may object to this or count it merely a narrow and private view of truth, let me say God has set His hallmark of approval upon this message from Paul's day to the present. Whether stated in these exact words or not, this has been the content of all preaching that has brought life and power to the world through the centuries. The mystics, the reformers, the revivalists have put their emphasis here, and signs and wonders and mighty operations of the Holy Ghost gave witness to God's approval.

Dare we, the heirs of such a legacy of power, tamper with the truth? Dare we with our stubby pencils erase the lines of the blueprint or alter the pattern shown us in the Mount? May God forbid. Let us preach the old cross and we will know the old power. (**A. W. Tozer,** *Man, the Dwelling Place of God, 1966*)

Walking in the Supernatural Power of Prayer

The Unity that Releases Authority
by David Demian - Watchmen of the Nations

When most of us think of the word "unity" in the Church we think of coming together around godly goals. If an evangelist comes to our town to do a crusade, churches and ministries in the city will band together in support of this godly goal - seeing the lost saved. But while we work together, this does not necessarily translate into the unity that Jesus prayed for in [**John 17**]. We are simply bringing our influence and resources together to pursue a common goal and when that goal is completed, we each go back to our own lives/visions/ministries.

I think this happens because we wrongly assume unity is about amassing or collecting together our gifts/talents/authority/influence - adding them up to a greater collective strength. But I believe there is a spiritual power in unity that we need to understand.

The Power of Unity

"Now the whole world had one language and a common speech. Then they said, 'Come, let us build ourselves a city, with a tower that reaches to the heavens, so that we may make a name for ourselves and not be scattered over the face of the whole earth.

'But the LORD came down to see the city and the tower that the men were building.

The LORD said, "If as one people speaking the same language they have begun to do this, then nothing they plan to do will be impossible for them. Come, let us go down and confuse their language so they will not understand each other." So the LORD scattered them from there over all the earth, and they stopped building the city. That is why it was called Babel--because there the LORD confused the language of the whole world. From there the LORD scattered them over the face of the whole earth". [**Genesis 11:1;4-9**]

If a people can come to the place of speaking with one language, one voice, nothing will be impossible for them. At the tower of Babel, the people tapped into this power but because they were operating under their own will and not in submission to the Lord, this power could have been very destructive. So God intervened and shattered their communication - their ability to come into one voice.

Walking in the Supernatural Power of Prayer

If people unsubmitted to God could wield such power, imagine the power of unity that is available to the Church that walks as Jesus spoke about in [**John 17**] - in a oneness that mirrors that of the Father and the Son?

"And when the day of Pentecost was fully come, they were all with one accord in one place. And suddenly there came a sound from heaven as of a rushing mighty wind, and it filled all the house where they were sitting. And there appeared unto them cloven tongues like as of fire, and it sat upon each of them.
And they were all filled with the Holy Ghost, and began to speak with other tongues, as the Spirit gave them utterance. And there were dwelling at Jerusalem Jews, devout men, out of every nation under heaven. Now when this was noised abroad, the multitude came together, and were confounded, because that every man heard them speak in his own language" [**Acts 2:1-6**]

I believe what happened in Acts 2 was God's divine redemption and restoration of the true unity that had been defiled by human will at Babel. At the very foundational moment of the church God gathered 120 in the upper room to wait upon Him. Unlike the people at the Tower of Babel, they were not trying by their own strength to reach their own goals. They were simply submitted to the Lord and waiting for the promise of the Holy Spirit. As they did, they experienced a supernatural visitation where the Holy Spirit filled them. As they spoke only what the Spirit gave them to speak, the Lord supernaturally enabled all the people around them to hear the same message - God being praised - each in their own language. For the first time since Babel, the power of true unity was realized and the result was a harvest of 3000 souls and an explosion of the church in a single day.

Why Is Unity So Important?

I believe what we see in the story of [**Acts 2**] was a radical shift as God began the process of establishing His kingdom in the Church. The disciples had already experienced spiritual authority *as individuals* - they had been sent to heal the sick, cast out demons, preach the gospel. They had seen signs, wonders and miracles - the power of God displayed.

After the crucifixion and resurrection, for 40 days Jesus appeared to them teaching about the kingdom of God [**Acts 1:3**] The Day of Pentecost came and with it the birthing of the kingdom model of the church- one body, united in submission and following One Voice, being empowered by the Holy Spirit and walking in an authority that eludes the church today. Why? Because I believe the church of Acts operated in the power of *corporate anointing*, birthed from their unity, that we have not yet seen fully restored in the church today. Unity is one of the keys of end time revival as Jesus spoke about in [**John 17**] and that is why the enemy has fought it with all his might.

May they be brought to complete unity to let the world know that you sent me and have loved them even as you have loved me. [**John 17:23**]

Authority 101

We understand that in a home, a husband and wife who are walking in agreement and unity have the authority to see God's purposes fulfilled in their family. In a church or a ministry, if the leadership team walks in unity they have authority in that church or ministry. Now if a couple on a church board have unity in their home, does that mean they have the authority to bring forth the purposes of God for their church, even if the rest of the board is not in agreement one with another? No, this couple has to be in agreement with others in the leadership team to see God's purposes fully fulfilled for the church.

Does this take away the sovereignty of God? By no means. God can still at any time exercise His sovereign right to do as He chooses. But overall, He has set laws of the kingdom in place and has chosen to bind His will to His word. The laws of seedtime and harvest (sowing and reaping), the principles of faith are kingdom laws, even as there are principles about authority and about unity.

True Corporate Authority

In many ways the church is still functioning in an Old Testament model when it comes to *authority*. In the Old Testament, God would anoint an individual - a prophet, a priest or a king - who would be given the authority by the Lord to lead. But as we saw in the book of Acts, at the inception of the church the Spirit of God rested not on one man but on a corporate body of 120.

So as we move more into a model of the kingdom, we should expect to see a *body of believers*, carrying the same spirit, passion and heart that will rise in unity to walk together. I believe the early church walked in a revelation of this *corporate anointing*. But over time, as religious rules replaced relationship with God and one another, the church entered a period where many truths the Lord had poured in at

Walking in the Supernatural Power of Prayer

its inception were lost, including this principle of corporate unity that releases authority.

And so today although the church has the potential to exercise an authority to address power and principalities at city, region or nation-wide levels, we have not yet seen this authority *demonstrated*. But that is because no one individual, ministry, or denomination, no matter how anointed they are, no matter how much revelation they have, can exercise this level of authority alone. It is a *corporate authority that is required that can only be released through true unity.*

Since Martin Luther re-established the foundation of salvation by grace we have been in an age of restoration in the church. Wave after wave of truth - baptism, holiness, the infilling of the Holy Spirit, healing, prophecy have all been restored to the church. And I believe now is the time when God wants to open to us a revelation of the power of unity to release authority that He might re-establish the government of God in His church and by extension, in the nation.

"His intent was that now, through the church, the manifold wisdom of God should be made known to the rulers and authorities in the heavenly realms, according to his eternal purpose which he accomplished in Christ Jesus our Lord" [**Ephesians 3:10-11**]

Corporate Death Precedes Unity

What is the key to corporate unity? I believe it's when we realize that true unity is not found in collective human strength or giftedness but from collective death and humility and brokenness that brings us into a place of submission to the Lord and to one another.

As believers, most of us understand that our commitment to Christ means dying to our own desires and wants that we might live like Jesus lived, in total submission to the will of the Father.

I have been crucified with Christ and I no longer live, but Christ lives in me. The life I live in the body, I live by faith in the Son of God, who loved me and gave himself for me. [**Galatians 2:20**]

But there is another level of death and submission that we must enter into if we are going to truly walk corporately together as one body in submission to One Head. This is what Jesus exemplified in the way He walked - total submission to the Father. Jesus did not do anything except what He would see the Father doing and He would not speak anything that he didn't hear the Father speaking.

So if we want to come to this place as a body, who really listen only to One Voice and gives the Lord the pleasure to direct us exactly as He wants, then we need to come to the place of being willing to die even to the gifts and visions the Lord has given us. It's not about laying down our giftings and not using them, but it's about dying to our right to use our gifts to build our own vision or ministry. It's not about canceling what we do but it's about allowing the Holy Spirit to channel it for the corporate when and how He sees fit. Only when we come to this place will He truly be One Head over one body, His church.

The Trinity Test

The key is to gather a critical mass of believers not to mingle their giftings, experiences and abilities to build something but to lay down and die to their own.

The power of that kind of unity resembles that of a nuclear power.

The first nuclear explosion in history took place in New Mexico, at the Alamogordo Test Range, on the Jornada del Muerto (Journey of Death) desert, in the test named Trinity.

The Trinity test in the Journey of Death desert? A few months before the test a platform of 108 tons (almost 242,000 pounds) of TNT (dynamite) was blown up in order to calibrate the instruments that would measure the force of the atomic blast. The plutonium core that powered the bomb was the size of a large briefcase.

And the atomic blast? It blew out all the instruments - it was stronger than anything that could be measured.

I believe this is an amazing picture of the power of true unity. A critical mass is the minimum amount of fissionable material required to sustain a nuclear fission reaction. If a critical mass **(remnant)** of believers will humble themselves to walk in true unity they can operate in a spiritual authority far more powerful than any amassing of human strengths or influence can provide.

~ So the key is us ~

bringing our strengths, but **"laying down our crowns" at the feet of the Lord Jesus**. We submit ourselves as a corporate body to seek the Lord together, refusing to move until He speaks. And once we have heard Him and come into the agreement of a clear witness (it seems right to us and the Holy Spirit) as to His direction and timings, then will we begin to move with the authority of Heaven to address principalities and powers over our cities, regions and nations.

A New Age in the Church

The detonation of the Atomic bomb ushered the world into a new era - the Atomic Age. It shifted the balance of power in the Second World War, bringing it to a rapid conclusion. And it changed the face of warfare, forever.

I believe that today we are standing on the brink of such an equally radical transformation. The "Trinity Test" happened in the book of Acts. But now it's time for us to enter fully into the new era - the Age of the Kingdom - and experience the full restoration of what the Lord intended for the church that began on the Day of Pentecost. We will not be able to walk in the demonstrated fear of the Lord, the great signs and wonders and miracles, the deep bond of love and community, the great grace that was in the Early Church - without a true revelation of and commitment to the unity of the body that will release true corporate authority. May God prepare the church to be the glorious Bride for her Soon-Coming King!

Walking in the Supernatural Power of Prayer

Effectual Fervent Prayer

Text: James 5:16

Prayer does not equip you for greater works.
Prayer is the greater work. ---- by **Oswald Chambers**

As mature Christians we are naive to ignore or deny the reality of spiritual conflicts between good and evil and our role in them as believing saints. Our main weapon in a prayer offensive is a keen knowledge and application of scripture "declared verbally" in the same way Jesus fought the devil in his wilderness experience.

1. Prayer is a vital key that connects us with our heavenly Father.

2. Prayer is both an incredible privilege and an awesome responsibility. It can move the hand of God in situations where there is no other hope.

3. Biblical prayer is crying to God out of the depths; it is the pouring out of the soul before God.

4. "Prayer is like the dove that Noah sent forth, which blessed him not only when it returned with an olive-leaf in its mouth, but when it never returned at all."

[**James 5:16**] The effectual fervent prayer of a righteous man availeth much.

- When a person is RIGHT with God, the power of his sincere prayer is tremendous!"

- The conditions for that promise: "when a person is right with God and prays sincerely".

- Effectual fervent prayer is the hardest kind of work there is to do. Not only does it take more out of a person than any other kind of work, we have to handle ourselves with a strong discipline to make time for effectual fervent prayer.

I. Our natural tendency is to shrink back when it comes to praying for the impossible.
A. The problem is that we rest the power of prayer too much upon ourselves.
B. **We think that we are the ones making things happen in prayer.**
C. **Instead we are to see ourselves as instruments in the Lord's hands for accomplishing his purposes through prayer.**
D. <u>Prayer is an act of obedience and privilege for the believer.</u>
E. <u>We are commanded to pray.</u> But we <u>are also invited to bring our needs before the Lord.</u>
F. We are to anchor ourselves in his faithfulness and promises.
G. We are to see that the very fact that God commands us to pray is a foundation for effectiveness in our prayers

II. We hesitate to pray, thinking that it will do no good, but James calls our attention once again to the means God has established for doing his work among us—prayer. Do you believe this? We are so accustomed to neglecting prayer that it is hard for us to think of its power through God among us.

Walking in the Supernatural Power of Prayer

The Power of Fervent Prayer

A. Peter was in prison awaiting his execution. The Church had neither human power nor influence to save him. There was no earthly help, but there was help to be obtained by the way of Heaven. They gave themselves to fervent, importunate prayer. God sent His angel, who aroused Peter from sleep and led him out through the first and second wards of the prison; and when they came to the iron gate, it opened to them of its own accord, and Peter was free.

B. 'Prayer has divided seas, rolled up flowing rivers, made rocks gush into fountains, quenched flames of fire, muzzled lions, disarmed vipers and poisons, marshaled the stars against the wicked, stopped the course of the moon, arrested the sun in its rapid race, burst open iron gates, released souls from eternity, conquered the strongest devils, commanded legions of angels down from heaven. Prayer has bridled and chained the raging passions of man and routed and destroyed vast armies of proud, daring, blustering atheists. Prayer has brought one man from the bottom of the sea and carried another in a chariot of fire to heaven. What has prayer not done?'

What is it that makes our prayer effectual (or effective)?

1. Fervent prayer is putting your whole self---all of your attention, your mind, your will, and your emotions---on that thing you're praying about. That means your mind is focused on prayer instead of drifting off on other things. Fervent prayer will make a difference in the lives of people, but we must understand that it takes an effort and a sacrifice of our time.

2. In [**Matthew 15:22-28**], the Canaanite woman would not take no for an answer. She asked for her daughter's healing, and three times she was rejected. But she wouldn't give up. She understood the heart and character of the Lord Jesus. She not only received the healing of her daughter, but was commended by Jesus: "Woman, you have great FAITH!"

3. James gives us Elijah as the example of effective prayer in action (**see verses 17-18**). What gave Elijah the boldness to pray that the rain would stop, and then, at his word, start again? [*1 Kings 17:1; 18:41-45*].

• Elijah's prayer was BASED ON THE WORD OF GOD!

All of Israel had turned away from the Lord to worship Baal, the idol-god of a cruel heathen religion. Up stands one solitary man, a total unknown, and boldly proclaims to the king that "there will be neither dew nor rain in the next few years except at my word!'' But his authority was based on a promise and warning found in [**Deuteronomy 11:13-17**]:

4. Daniel also Discovered the Secret

In [**Daniel 9:3-19**]. Daniel poured out his heart in prayer before God that his people, who had been taken out of their homeland and held as captives in Babylon, would return to their land. The basis of his prayer can be seen in verse 2:

" . . . I, Daniel, understood from the Scriptures, according to the word of the Lord given to Jeremiah the prophet, that the desolation of Jerusalem would last seventy years''.

The Lord had spoken right at the time when Judah had gone into captivity that they would be in Babylon for 70 years [**Jeremiah 25:11-12**]. Daniel, reading the Scriptures one day, came across that promise and realized that the 70-year period was almost completed. However, he didn't just sit back and wait for God to do it. Daniel began to PRAY that what God had promised would be fulfilled. The Lord has chosen to give us the privilege and responsibility of being involved with Him in His purposes on earth. Daniel lived to see his people return!

Walking in the Supernatural Power of Prayer

• **Effectual prayer, then, is prayer that is based on God's Word.**

When we know the promises that He has given, and understand His character and the principles by which He works as revealed in His Word,

we can pray with confidence and authority, knowing that our prayers will be answered.

Walking in the Supernatural Power of Prayer

• Pray According to God's Will
By Watchman Nee

"I anticipated the dawning of the morning, and cried: I hoped in thy words. Mine eyes anticipated the night watches, that I might meditate on thy word." [**Ps. 119.147,148**]

"In the third year of Cyrus King of Persia, a thing was revealed unto Daniel, whose name was called Belteshazzar; and the thing was true, even a great warfare: and he understood the thing, and had understanding of the vision. In those days I, Daniel, was mourning three whole weeks. I ate no pleasant bread, neither came flesh nor wine into my mouth, neither did I anoint myself at all, till three whole weeks were fulfilled . . . Then said he unto me, Fear not, Daniel; for from the first day that thou didst set thy heart to understand, and to humble thyself before thy God, thy words were heard: and I am come for thy words' sake. But the prince of the kingdom of Persia withstood me one and twenty days . . . Then said he, Knowest thou wherefore I am come unto thee? and now will I return to fight with the prince of Persia: and when I go forth, lo, the prince of Greece shall come. But I will tell thee that which is inscribed in the writing of truth . . . "
[**Dan. 10.1-21**]

As we read Daniel chapter 10 which tells us of how Daniel prayed, we should notice at least two points.

Point One

The first point to be noticed is that one who really prays is a person who not only often approaches God but also whose will frequently enters into God's will—that is to say, his thought often enters into God's thought. This is a most important principle in prayer. There is a kind of prayer which originates entirely from our need. Though at times the Lord hears such prayers, He nonetheless gets little or nothing out of them. Please take note of this verse: *"He gave them their request, but sent leaness into their soul"* [**Ps. 106.15**]. What does this passage mean? As Israel cried to God for the gratification of their lust, He did answer them by indeed giving them what they asked for—but with the result, however, of their being weakened before Him. Oh yes, sometimes God will hear and respond to your prayers for the sake of satisfying your own needs, yet His own will is not fulfilled. Let us see that such prayer does not have much value in it.

But there is another kind of prayer, which comes out of God's own need. It is of God, and it is initiated by God. And such prayer is most valuable. In order to have such prayer, the one who prays must not only personally often appear before God but also he must allow his will to enter into God's will, his thought must be allowed to enter into God's thought. Since he habitually lives in the Lord's presence, such a person is given to know His will and thoughts. And these divine wills and thoughts quite naturally become his own desires, which he then expresses in prayer.

Oh how we must learn this second kind of prayer. Although we are immature and weak, we may nevertheless approach God and let His Spirit bring our will into God's will and our thought into God's thought. As we touch a little of His will and thought we come to understand a little more of how He works and what He requires of us. So that gradually the will and thought of God which we have known and entered into becomes in us our prayer. And such prayer is of great value.

Having entered into God's thought and thus having touched His will and purpose, Daniel found in his own heart the same desire as God's. The longing of God was reproduced in Daniel and became Daniel's desire.

So that when he expressed this desire in prayer with cries and groanings, he was actually articulating God's desire. We need to have this kind of prayer, for it really touches the divine heart. We do not need more words; what we need is a touching more of the Lord's mind. Let the Spirit of God lead us into the intent of God's heart.

Walking in the Supernatural Power of Prayer

Of course, this kind of prayer will require time to learn. In the beginning of such a learning process let us not seek for more words nor for more thoughts. Our spirit should be calm and restful. We may bring our current situation to the Lord and consider it in the light of His countenance, or we may forget our present condition and simply meditate on His word before Him. Or we may just live before Him and try to touch Him with our spirit. As a matter of fact, it is not we who go forth to meet God but it is God who is waiting there for us. And there in His presence we perceive something and touch upon the will of God. The greatest wisdom comes, in fact, from this very source. By this, our will enters into His will and our thought enters into His heart. And from there our prayer will rise to Him.

As we bring our will and thought to God His own will and thought begin to be reproduced in us, and then this becomes our will and thought. This kind of prayer is most valuable and full of weight. Let us recall what the Lord Jesus said about prayer: *"After this manner therefore pray ye: Our Father who art in heaven, hallowed by thy name. Thy kingdom come. Thy will be done, as in heaven, so on earth"* [**Matt. 6.9,10**]. These are not just three words for us to repeat. These words, which disclose the will and thought of God, are to be reproduced in us when the Spirit of God brings our mind to God. And as they become our will and thought, the prayer which we afterwards utter is most valuable and most weighty.

Over the one and the same matter there is the possibility of having two different kinds of prayer. One kind has its source in our own will. It is based on our own thinking and our own expectations.

The Lord may hear and answer our prayer, but such prayer has a very low value attached to it. If, on the other hand, we bring this matter before God and let His Spirit merge our will into God's will and our thought into God's thought, we shall discover within us a deep longing which is in fact a reproduction of His will and thought. Suppose the Lord is grieved and mournful over the death of men. We too will develop such a burden of not willing to see even one soul perish. And such is a reproduction of God's heart which enables us to pray with inward sighings. Or if the Lord is anxious and hurt because of the failure of His children, this very same burden will be reproduced in us; with the result that we will have the same yearning of not willing to see a child of God fall into sin and darkness. Then prayer and intercession will issue forth from within us. There we will confess, plead for forgiveness, and ask God to purify His children.

Hence one kind of prayer is prayed according to our own will; the other kind is prayed as the will of God which has been reproduced in us and has become our will. How different are these two kinds of prayer. In the latter case, as any believer approaches God, the will of God will be reproduced in him. It will become his breath and his sigh. And prayer which is prayed according to this will has worth and weight.

God has many things to do on earth, touching many areas. How, then, can we ever pray according to our own feeling and thought? We should draw near to God and allow Him to impress us with what He desires to do so that we ourselves may intercede with groanings. In case, as we approach Him, God puts His will of spreading the gospel in us, this soon will become a burden in us. And when we pray according to that burden, we shall have a sense as though our very sigh is divulging the will of God. The Lord may put a variety of wills or reproduce a variety of burdens in us. But whatever be the particular will or burden, whenever it is reproduced in a person's heart, that person is able to make the Lord's will his own will and pray it out accordingly. When, in the case of Daniel, he came before God, he touched a certain matter; and then we saw that he prayed out that thing with deep groanings. How precious and substantial is prayer such as this. It can hallow God's name, bring in God's kingdom, and cause God's will to prevail on earth as in heaven.

Walking in the Supernatural Power of Prayer

Point Two

The **second point** to be noticed is, that when we pray with such prayer, our prayer will shake up hell and affect Satan. For this reason, Satan will rise up to hinder such prayer. **All prayers which come from God touch the powers of darkness.** <u>Here involves spiritual warfare.</u>

Perhaps our physical bodies, our families, or whatever pertains to us will be attacked by Satan. For whenever there is such prayer, it calls forth Satanic assault. The enemy so attacks in order that our prayer might be discontinued. He may even try to throw up some blockage in the air so as to delay the answer to prayer. That prayer ought to receive a response quickly; however, the answer seems to be suspended in the air. In just such fashion as this, the answer to Daniel's prayer was hindered for twenty-one days although God actually heard him the day he began to pray. In such a situation, what did Daniel do? He knelt before God and he waited until the answer to prayer arrived.

Let me ask this question: Do you ever wonder why your prayer remains unanswered? Perhaps it is suspended somewhere, still within the period of twenty one days! The answer of the throne may possibly have been given, yet it encounters opposition and, consequently, is suspended in air. Why? It awaits more prayers on earth; it needs people who will patiently and humbly wait upon God.

Oh do draw near to God's presence, calm down before Him, lay aside your own thoughts, and enter into His thought. You will then realize the significance of prayer and see in how many matters God is waiting for you to pray. Things around the entire world are to be subjects of your prayer, and matters in all directions are to be touched through your prayer. You do not pray according to your own feeling; you instead bring your own heart desire to the heart desire of God and let His will become your will, your groaning, and your hope in the universe.

Nothing of the will of God is ever released without passing through man, and nothing of whatever will of God released through man is ever free from an encounter with the power of Satan.

For the realization of God's will, there is the need for prayer; to remove Satan's opposition requires prayer. Let us exercise the authority of prayer in loosing whatever must be loosed and binding whatever should be bound. Let us not pray after our own will.

Let us draw near to God and pray according to the will which He has reproduced in us. When God says that this must be done we also say it must be done. When He says this must not exist, we too say it must not exist. We ought to forget ourselves, touch God's will, and express His current will through prayer.

(From the book *Let us Pray* by Watchman Nee)

• Prayer and God's Work
by Watchman Nee

"With all prayer and supplication praying at all seasons in the Spirit, and watching thereunto in all perseverance and supplication." (Eph. 6.18)

"Thus saith the Lord Jehovah: For this, moreover, will I be inquired of by the house of Israel, to do it for them: I will increase them with men like a flock."(Ezek. 36.37)

One

When God works, He does so with specific law and definite principle. Even though He could do whatever pleases Him, yet he never acts carelessly. He always performs according to His determinate law and principle. Unquestionably He can transcend all these laws and principles, for He is God and is quite capable of acting according to His own pleasure. Nonetheless, we discover a most marvelous fact in the Bible; which is, that in spite of His exceeding greatness and His ability to operate according to His will, God ever acts along the line of the law or principle which He has laid down. It seems as though He deliberately puts himself under the law to be controlled by His own law.

Now then, what is the principle of God's working? God's working has a primal principle behind it, which is, that He wants man to pray, that He desires man to cooperate with Him through prayer.
There was once a Christian who well knew how to pray. He declared this, that all spiritual works include four steps: The first step is that God conceives a thought, which is His will: The second step is that God reveals this will to His children through the Holy Spirit, causing them to know that He has a will, a plan, a demand and expectation: The third step is that God's children return His will by praying to Him, for prayer is responding to God's will—if our heart is wholly one with His heart, we will naturally voice in our prayer what He intends to do: And the fourth step is that God will accomplish this very thing.

Here we are concerned not with the first step nor with the second, but with the third step—how we are to return God's will by praying to Him. Please notice the word "return". All prayers with worth possess this element of return in them. If our prayer is only for the purpose of accomplishing our plan and expectations it does not have much value in the spiritual realm. Prayer must originate from God and be responded to by us. Such alone is meaningful prayer, since God's work is controlled by such prayer. How many things the Lord indeed desires to do, yet He does not perform them because His people do not pray. He will wait until men agree with Him, and then He will work. This is a great principle in God's working, and it constitutes one of the most important principles to be found in the Bible.

Two

The word in Ezekiel 36.37 is quite surprising. The Lord says He has a purpose, which is, that He will increase the house of Israel with men like a flock. This is the determinate will of God. What He ordains He will perform. Nevertheless, He will not accomplish it instantly but will wait awhile. What is the reason for the waiting? The Lord says, "For this, moreover, will I be inquired of by the house of Israel, to do it for them." He has decided to increase the house of Israel with men, but He must wait till the children of Israel inquire of Him about the matter. Let us see that even if He himself has resolved to perform certain things He will not do so immediately. He will wait until men show their agreement before He proceeds. Each time He works He never goes ahead immediately simply because He has His will; no, He will wait, if necessary, for His people to express their agreement in prayer before He does act. This assuredly is a most amazing phenomenon.

Walking in the Supernatural Power of Prayer

Let us always be mindful of this truth, that all spiritual works are decided by God and desired by His children—all are initiated by God and approved by His children. This is a great principle in spiritual work. "For this, moreover, will I be inquired of by the house of Israel," says the Lord. His work awaits the inquiring of the children of Israel. And one day the Israelites really inquired, and without delay He performed it for them.

Do we see this principle of God's work? After He has initiated something, He pauses in its execution until we pray. Since the time of the founding of the church, there is nothing God does on earth without the prayer of His children. From the moment He has His children, He does everything according to the prayer of His own. He puts everything in their prayer. We do not know why He acts in such a way; but we do know that this is a fact. God is willing to condescend himself to such a position of taking delight in fulfilling His will through His children.

There is another illustration of this in Isaiah 62: *"I have set watchmen upon thy walls, O Jerusalem; they shall never hold their peace day or night: ye that are Jehovah's remembrancers, take ye no rest, and give him no rest, till he establish, and till he make Jerusalem a praise in the earth"* (v.6,7). God intends to make Jerusalem a praise in the earth. How does He realize it? He sets watchmen upon its walls that they may cry to Him. How should they cry? *"Take ye no rest, and give him no rest"*—we are to cry to Him unceasingly and give Him no rest. We keep on praying until He accomplishes His work. Although the Lord has already willed to make Jerusalem a praise in the earth, He nonetheless sets watchmen on its walls. By their prayer will He perform. He urges them not to pray just once, but to pray without ceasing. Keep on praying till His will is done. In other words, the will of God is governed by the prayers of man. The Lord waits for us to pray. Let us understand clearly that as regards the content of God's will it is entirely decided by God himself; we do not make, nor even participate in, the decision. Yet concerning the doing of His will it is governed by our prayer.

A brother once observed that God's will is like a train whereas our prayer is like the rails of a train. A train may travel to any place, except that it must run on rails. It has tremendous power to go east, west, south and north, but it can only run to places where rails have been laid. So that it is not because God has no power (He, like a train, has power, great power); but because He chooses to be governed by man's prayer, therefore all valuable prayers (like a train's rails) pave the way for God. Consequently, if we do not take up the responsibility of prayer, we will hinder the fulfillment of God's will.

Three

When God created man He gave him a free will. There thus exist in the universe three different wills; namely, the will of God, the will of Satan the enemy, and the will of man. People may wonder why the Lord does not destroy Satan in a moment's time. The Lord could, but He has not done so. And why? Because He wants man to cooperate with Him in dealing with Satan. Now God has His will, Satan has his, and man has his too. God seeks to have man's will joined with His. He will not destroy Satan all by himself. We do not know entirely why God has chosen this way, but we do know He delights in doing it this way—namely, that He will not act independently; He looks for the cooperation of man. And this is the responsibility of the church on earth.

When the Lord wishes to do a thing He first puts His own thought in us through the Holy Spirit. Only after we have turned this thought into prayer will He perform it. Such is the procedure of divine working; God will not work out anything in any other way. He needs the cooperation of us men. He needs a will that is one with His will and is sympathetic to Him. If God does everything without involving us men, then there is absolutely no need for us to be here on earth, nor do we need to know what His will is. Yet every will of God must be done by us, since He calls for our will to be one with His own.

Thus the first step in our doing God's will is for us to utter His will in prayer. God's will is uttered through our prayer. Here may we see that prayer is indeed a work. There is no work more important than prayer because the latter accomplishes as well as expresses the will of God. Hence all prayer which comes out of self-will is useless. Prayers which are in accordance with God's will originate from God, are revealed to us by the Holy Spirit, and

Walking in the Supernatural Power of Prayer

return to God through prayers. Whatever prayer is in accordance with God's will must begin with God's will; men merely respond to, and transmit, this will. All which commence with us are prayers of no spiritual worth.

As we read through church history, we may notice that every great revival has always come from prayer. This shows us how prayer enables the Lord to do what He desires to do. We cannot ask Him to do what He does not want to do, though we may certainly delay what He wishes to do. God is absolute; therefore, we cannot change Him, neither can we force Him to do what He does not want to do, nor can we persuade Him not to do what He wants to do. Even so, when we are called to be the channel of His will we may doubtless block God's work if we do not cooperate with Him.

For this reason, our prayer should never be asking the Lord to do what He has no desire to do or trying to change His will. It is simply a praying out of His will, thus enabling Him to do what He desires to do. In case we beg strongly with the expectation of forcing Him to do that which He has no intention of doing, we are wasting our effort, for our prayer is of no avail. If God is not willing to act, who can make Him act? One thing only can we do, and that is, we can pray out what God has desired. Then will He accomplish His work because we are one with Him.

Take, as an example, the coming of the Holy Spirit on the day of Pentecost. Hundreds of years before the day of Pentecost, even at the time of Joel, God had already mentioned this coming. But the Holy Spirit came down only after many disciples had gathered and prayed. Although the advent of the Spirit had long before been determined by God, it did not come to pass until people had prayed. The Lord is capable of doing many things; yet He likes to do them after men have prayed. He is waiting for our consent. He himself is already willing, but He wants us to be willing too. How many are the things He has decided to do, and yet He waits, because we have not expressed to Him our agreement. May we see that although we cannot force God to do what He does not want to do, we nevertheless can certainly ask Him to do what He undoubtedly wants to do. Frequently we miss spiritual blessing because we fail to express God's will in prayer.

If anyone will rise up and devote himself to the work of prayer exclusively, how excellent that will be. God is waiting for such ones to work together with Him so as to enable Him to finish His work. Some Christians may ask why the Lord does not save more sinners, why He does not cause every believer to overcome. I sincerely believe that He would undoubtedly do such works if people would only pray. He is not unwilling to work, He simply wants first to obtain a people who will work together with Him. Whenever people begin working with Him, He performs immediately. In all spiritual works, the Lord is always waiting for an expression of desire from His children. Whether or not a matter is done is dependent upon how His children pray. We therefore ought to declare our cooperation with Him. God is waiting to bless us. The question now is: Will we pray?

Those who do not know God may retort on this wise: If God wants to do something, why does He not just do it, why should He desire men to pray? Is He not all knowing? Will God not be annoyed by much prayer? Let us keep in mind, however, that we humans are free-will beings. As the Lord cannot deny His own will, so He will not coerce ours. He will wait for us if His will is not prayed forth by us. Yet does He not want His will to be done on earth as it is in heaven? Why then does He not go ahead and perform it? Why does the Lord ask His disciples to pray: "Our Father who art in heaven,... thy will be done, as in heaven, so on earth"? If He wants His kingdom to come, why does it not come automatically? Why must the disciples pray, "Thy kingdom come"? Why, if God doubtless desires His name to be hallowed by all men, does He not make it so by himself instead of His requiring the disciples to pray: "Hallowed be thy name"? All this is for no other reason than the fact that God himself does not wish to do anything independently, because He chooses to have men cooperate with Him. He has the power, but He needs our prayers to lay the tracks down for the train of His will to run on. The more tracks we lay, the more abundant will be the works of God. Our prayers should therefore serve the purpose of laying down a huge spiritual network of railroad tracks. And the more the better.

Walking in the Supernatural Power of Prayer

Four

How should we lay tracks for the will of God? The answer: *"With all prayer and supplication praying at all seasons in the Spirit"* (Eph. 6.18). Our prayer should touch in many directions. We should pray constantly. Pray specific prayers as well as general ones. Many of our prayers are too thinly spread; there are too many holes by which Satan is given plenty of opportunities to slip in. Were our prayers well-rounded and tightly guarded, he would have no chance to do havoc.

When, for example, a brother goes out to preach you should lay rails for him so that God's will might be fulfilled in him. If you pray only a few words of general prayer, asking the Lord to bless him, protect him, and supply his needs, such a prayer net is too thinly spread. If you want to pray for a particular person you should spread for him a very tight net so that Satan can find no hole through which to creep in. How, then, ought you to pray? As the brother in question is preparing to leave, you should pray for his health, his luggage, the train he will ride, even the time of the train, his rest and food on the train, and people he will meet on the train. You should also pray for everything he will be involved in after he disembarks: pray for the place where he will stay, pray for the neighbors, even pray for the things he will read, also pray for his work—the time involved in it as well as all other things connected with the work. If you pray for him as extensively as this, it will be most difficult for Satan to find a loophole through which to attack him. The work of prayer is therefore a real work. All who are lazy, foolish, and careless cannot do such work. Yet how often, when there are those who earnestly and extensively pray for a certain thing, the thing is found to be done.

There is another lesson we should learn here. Satan is so full of wiles that it is really hard for us to outguess him. We are unable to pray over every last detail, and hence we can only pray in this manner: *"O Lord, may Your precious blood answer whatever comes from Satan."* Let us realize that the precious blood of Christ is the answer to all the works of the enemy. Such prayer is the best one that can be offered against him, so that he can never get through this net to assault God's people.

Each time we pray, we need to see three aspects: first, we must see to whom we are praying; second, we must know for whom we pray; and third, we ought to realize against whom we are praying. Frequently we only remember two aspects of prayer—those concerning God (to whom we pray) and men (for whom we pray). And thus we have overlooked the enemy aspect. In this matter of prayer we should know not only to whom we pray but also against whom we pray. We should know for whom we pray but we should also know that there is an enemy who lurks around to hurt us. Our prayer is directed towards God, for men, and against Satan. If we take care of these three aspects, God will surely work for us.

Everyone who truly works for the Lord must spread the net of prayer so that He may work through that person. God is not at all unwilling to work: He is simply waiting for people to pray. How He waits expectantly for men to have a prayer life, how His will awaits the prayers of men. Oftentimes, without your setting a time for prayer beforehand, you sense a burden to pray. This indicates that there is one item in God's will which requires your prayer. Pray when you feel the burden of prayer—this is praying according to God's will. It is the Holy Spirit who constrains you to pray out the prayer which is in accordance with the will of God. When the Holy Spirit is urging you to pray, you should do so. If you do not pray, you will feel suffocated within as if there is something left undone. In the event you still do not pray, you will feel even more weighed down. Finally, if you do not pray at all, the spirit of prayer as well as the burden of prayer will be so dulled that it will be difficult for you to regain such feeling and to pray the prayer according to God's will afterwards.

Walking in the Supernatural Power of Prayer

Each time God puts a prayer thought into us His Holy Spirit first moves us into having a burden to pray for that particular matter. As soon as we receive such feeling we should immediately give ourselves to prayer. We should pay the cost of praying well for this matter. For when we are moved by the Holy Spirit our own spirit instantly senses a burden as though something were being laid upon our heart. After we pray it out we feel relieved as though having a heavy stone removed from off us. But in case we do not pour it out in prayer, we will get the feeling of something not yet done. If we do not pray it out we are not in harmony with God's heart. Were we to be faithful in prayer, that is to say, were we to pray as soon as the burden comes upon us, prayer would not become a weight, it would instead be light and pleasant.

What a pity that so many people quench the Holy Spirit here. They quench the sensation which the Holy Spirit gives to move them to pray. Hereafter, few of such sensations will ever come upon them. Thus they are no longer useful vessels before the Lord. The Lord can achieve nothing through them since they are no longer able to breathe out in prayer the will of God. Oh, if ever we fall to such an extent of having no prayer burden, we will have sunk indeed into a most perilous situation, for we have already lost communion with God and He is no more able to use us in His work. For this reason, we must be extra careful in dealing with the feeling which the Holy Spirit gives to us. Whenever there is a prayer burden we should immediately inquire of the Lord, saying, *"O God, what do you want me to pray for? What is it which you wish to accomplish that needs me to pray?"* And were we to pray it out, we would be entrusted by God with the next prayer. If our first burden is not yet discharged, we are unable to take up the second load.

Let us ask the Lord to make us faithful prayer partners. As soon as the burden comes, we have it discharged by praying it out. If the burden grows too heavy and it cannot be discharged by prayer, then we should fast. When prayer cannot discharge a burden, fasting must follow. Through fasting, the burden of prayer may quickly be discharged, since fasting is able to help us discharge the heaviest of burdens.

If anyone should continue on in performing the work of prayer, he will become a channel for the will of God. Whenever the Lord has anything to do, He will seek that person out. Let me say this, that the will of God is always in search of a way out. The Lord is always apprehending someone or some people to be the expression of His will. If many will rise up to do this work, He will do many things because of their prayers.

(From the book *Let us Pray* by Watchman Nee)

• Motives for Revival
by Dr. Martyn Lloyd-Jones

"And Moses said unto the Lord, See, thou sayest unto me, Bring up this people: and thou hast not let me know whom thou wilt send with me. Yet thou hast said, I know thee by name, and thou hast also found grace in my sight. Now therefore, I pray thee, if I have found grace in thy sight, shew me now the way, that I may know thee, that I may find grace in thy sight: and consider that this nation is thy people. And he said, My presence shall go with thee, and I will give thee rest. And he said unto him, If thy presence go not with me, carry us not up hence. For wherein shall it be known here that I and thy people have found grace in thy sight? is it not in that thou goest with us? so shall we be separated, I and thy people, from all the people that are upon the face of the earth. And the Lord said unto Moses, I will do this thing also that thou hast spoken: for thou hast found grace in my sight, and I know thee by name."—
[**Exodus 33:12-17**]

F you read the history of the great revivals of the past, you will find that—as you read of the men whom God has used most signally, as you study them in the period before the revival came, when they were pleading and interceding—you will find invariably that they were animated by exactly the same motives as we find here in the case of Moses. So we must be perfectly clear with regard to this matter of our motives.

I am calling you to pray for revival. Yes, but why should you pray for revival? Why should anybody pray for revival?

The answer that is first given here is this: a concern for the glory of God. You will find it at the end of verse **13**: *"Now therefore, I pray thee, if I have found grace in thy sight, shew me now thy way, that I may know thee, that I may find grace in thy sight; and consider that this nation is thy people."* That is the motive. That is the reason. Moses was concerned primarily about the glory of God. Now, you will find that he constantly used this particular argument with God…He is concerned about the name and, as it were, the reputation and the glory of God. That is the point he is making here again. *"This nation,"* he says, *"is thy people."* He is saying, in effect, that God's honor and God's glory is involved in this situation. They are, after all, His people: they have claimed that, He has given indications of that—He has brought them out of Egypt in a marvelous and a miraculous manner. He has brought them through the Red Sea; is He going to leave them here in the wilderness? What will the Egyptians say? What will the other nations say? Has He failed? He promised them great things; can He not execute them? Can He not bring them to fulfillment? Moses is suggesting to God that His own glory, His own honor, is involved in this whole situation…

This is what matters, is it not? The Church, after all, is the Church of God. *"She is His new creation, by water and word."* We are a people for God's own peculiar possession; and why has He called us out of darkness into His own marvelous light (**1Pe 2:9**)? Surely, it is that we may show forth His praises, His excellencies, His virtues.

Therefore, we should be concerned about this matter primarily because of the name, the glory, and the honor of God Himself. Whether we like it or not, it is a fact that the world judges God Himself, the Lord Jesus Christ, and the whole of the Christian faith by what it sees in us. We are His representatives; we are the people who take His name upon us; we are the people who talk about Him—and the man outside the Church regards the Church as the representative of God. Therefore, I argue that we must emulate1 the example of Moses as we find it here. Our first concern should be about the glory of God…Here is the thing, surely, that we must needs recapture. We are so subjective in our approach, always thinking about ourselves. That is not the way to pray for revival. **We must, in the first place, be concerned about God: His glory, His honor, His name.** This, to me, is essence of the whole matter.

Walking in the Supernatural Power of Prayer

Go through the great prayers of the Old Testament, and you will find it always there. These men had a passion for God; they were in trouble, they were unhappy because this great God was not being worshipped as He should be. And they prayed God for His own sake, for His glory's sake, to vindicate His own name and to arise and scatter His enemies. That is the first thing.

Then the second thing—and it must always come in the second place, never in the first—is a concern about the honor of the Church herself... It seems to me that there is no hope for revival until you and I, and all of us, have reached the stage in which we begin to forget ourselves a little and to be concerned for the Church, for God's body, His people here on earth. So many of our prayers are subjective and self-centered. We have our problems and difficulties; and by the time that we have finished with them, we are tired and exhausted, and we do not pray for the Church—[it is only] my blessing, my need, my this, my that. Now, I am not being hard and unkind; God has promised to deal with our problems. But where does the Church come into our prayers and intercessions? Do we go beyond our families and ourselves? We stand before the world and we say the only hope for the world is Christianity. We say the Church, and the Church alone, has the message that is needed...

Then, of course, the third reason is that Moses is concerned about the heathen that are outside. He wants them to know: *"For wherein shall it be known here [in the wilderness, where we are], that I and thy people have found grace in thy sight? is it not in that thou goest with us? so shall we be separated, I and thy people, from all the people that are upon the face of the earth"* [**Exo 33:16**].

These are the motives in praying for revival: for the name, honor, and glory of God, and for the sake of the Church that is His. Yes, and then for the sake of those people that are outside, that are scoffing, mocking, jeering, laughing, and ridiculing. *"Oh, God,"* say His people, one after another, *"arise and silence them. Do something so that we may be able to say to them, 'Be still, keep silent, give up.'"* *"Be still, and know that I am God"* [**Psa 46:10**]. That is the prayer of the people of God. They have their eye on those that are outside. You find illustrations of this right through the Bible. And this has been true of all men who have felt the burden of the condition of the Church, and whose hearts are breaking because they have seen the name of God blasphemed. Oh, you will find it in very strong language here in the Bible, sometimes so strong that certain little people are troubled by the imprecatory Psalms. But the imprecatory Psalms are just an expression of the zeal these men have for the glory of God. *"Let the sinners be consumed out of the earth,"* says the man in [**Psalm 104**]...It was not a desire for personal vengeance. It was that these men were consumed by a passion for God and His glory and His great name. There is something wrong with us if we do not feel this desire within us: that God should arise and do something that would shut the mouths and stop the tongues of these arrogant blasphemers of today, who speak with their mincing words upon radio and television—these supposed philosophers, these godless, arrogant men. Do we not feel, sometimes, this desire within us: that they might know that God is God and that He is the eternal God?...

This should make us ask, therefore, whether we are concerned at all about these people who are outside. It is a terrible state for the Church to be in, when she merely consists of a collection of very nice and respectable people who have no concern for the world, people who pass it by, drawing in their skirts in their horror at the bestiality, the foulness, and the ugliness of it all. We not only want the scoffers to be silenced; we should desire that these men and women, who are like sheep without a shepherd, might have their eyes opened, might begin to see the cause of their troubles and be delivered from the chains of iniquity and the shackles of infamy, vice, and foulness. Are we truly concerned about such people, and are we praying to God that He would do something, that they may be influenced and affected? There, as I understand it, are the three main motives that animated Moses as he offered up these petitions to God.

There is something else for us to notice, and that is the way in which he prayed. We have seen what he prayed for; we have seen why he prayed for it; now let us watch his method of prayer. If ever we needed instruction, it is just here. There are certain elements that always come out in all the great biblical prayers, and the first characteristic of

Walking in the Supernatural Power of Prayer

Moses' prayer is its boldness, its confidence. There is no hesitation here. There is a quiet confidence. Oh, let me use the term: there is a *"holy boldness."* This is the great characteristic of all prayers that have ever prevailed. It is, of course, inevitable. You cannot pray truly, still less can you intercede, if you have not an assurance of your acceptance, and if you do not know the way into the holiest of all. If, when you get down on your knees, you are reminded of your sins and are wondering what you can do about them; if you have to spend all your time praying for forgiveness and pardon, wondering whether God is listening or not—how can you pray? How can you intercede as Moses did here? No, Moses was face to face with God; he was assured; he was bold with a holy boldness. As we have seen, God had granted him intimations of His nearness, and so he was able to speak with this confidence and assurance…

But, there is a second point, which is most valuable and interesting, and that is the element of reasoning and of arguing that comes in. It is very daring, but it is very true. Let me remind you of it. *"Moses said unto the Lord, See..."*—which really means that he is arguing with God. *"See, thou sayest unto me, Bring up this people: and thou hast not let me know whom thou wilt send with me. Yet thou hast said..."* You see, he is reminding God of what He had said. He is having an argument with God: *"And yet thou hast said, I know thee by name, and thou hast also found grace in my sight. Now therefore,"* says Moses, as if he were saying to God, *"Be logical, be consistent, carry out your own argument. You cannot say this to me and then not do anything."* *"Now therefore, I pray thee, if..."*—still arguing—*"if I have found grace in thy sight, shew me now thy way, that I may know thee, that I may find grace in thy sight: and consider that this nation is thy people."* Then in **verse 16**, *"For, wherein"*—if you do not do this—*"wherein shall it be known here that I and thy people have found grace in thy sight? Is it not in that thou goest with us? so shall we be separated..."* He reasoned with God. He argued with God. He reminded God of His own promises, and he pleaded with God in the light of them. He said, *"Oh, God, can you not see that having said this you must...?"*

Is it right, someone may ask, to speak to God like that? Is this not presumption? No, these things go together. The author of the Epistle to the Hebrews, who talked so much about our going boldly to the throne of grace, at the same time reminds us that we do so always with reverence and with godly fear. This is all right. What is happening here is this: we are not seeing a man under the Law speaking to the Lawgiver. **No, it is a child here speaking to his father.** And the little child can take liberties with his father that a grown-up man, who is not his child, would not dare to take. Oh, yes, this is a child speaking, and he knows it. God has spoken to him, as it were, face to face; and Moses knows that. He comes with his love, his reverence, his godly fear, and he ventures to argue. He says, *"You have said this, therefore..."*

Another thing we should notice about prayer is its orderliness, its directness: the specific petition. Notice that Moses here does not offer up some vague, indefinite general prayer. No, he is concentrating on the one great need. Of course, he worshipped God; of course, there was the reverence and the godly fear, yes; but at this point, he concentrates on this one thing: this presence of God. He will not get away from it. He says, *"I will not move unless you come. You must come with us."* He gives his reasons and plies Him with all these arguments about it.

And if I may speak for myself, I shall not feel happy and encouraged until I feel that the Church is concentrating on this one thing: prayer for revival. But we have not come to it. We are still in the state of deciding in committees to do this, that, and the other, and asking God to bless what we have done. No, there is no hope along that line. It must be that one thing. We must feel this burden, **we must see this as the only hope, and we must concentrate on this, and we must keep on with it**—the orderliness, the arrangement, the concentration, the argument, and always the urgency. Moses here is as Jacob was in Genesis 32. This element always comes into true intercession. *"I will not let thee go,"* said Jacob. I am going on. The morning was breaking; he had been struggling through the night. *"Let me go."* *"No, I will not let thee go, except thou bless me."* There is the urgency. Read the great biblical prayers; it is always in them. In Acts 4, we read of the Christians asking God to act *"now!" "Oh God,"* they said, *"in the light of this, in our situation now: do this. Give us some indication, give us some signs, enable us to witness with this holy boldness, and to bear witness to the resurrection that they are prohibiting us to speak about."* See the urgency of the prayer. Moses keeps on coming back to it, repeating it, putting it in different forms

Walking in the Supernatural Power of Prayer

and from different angles. But there was just this one thing: *"If thy presence go not with me, carry us not up hence."* Insisting urgently, *"I will not let thee go."* There, it seems to me, are some of the lessons from this passage. We say our prayers, but have we ever prayed? Do we know anything about this encounter, this meeting? Have we the assurance of sins forgiven? Are we free from ourselves and self concern that we may intercede?

Have we a real burden for the glory of God and the name of the Church? Have we this concern for those who are outside? And are we pleading with God for His own name's sake because of His own promises to hear us and to answer us? Oh, my God, make of us intercessors such as Moses! It is no use anybody saying, "Ah, but he was an exceptionally great man." God, as we have seen in the history of revivals, has made use of men who are mere nobodies in exactly the same way as He used Moses here…It can be any one of us. May God make of us intercessors such as Moses was.

(From *Revival* by Dr. Martin Lloyd-Jones)

The First Great Awakening was marked

by united multi-church prayer meetings, and in Jonathan Edwards's writings he says that a key verse for those prayer meetings was[**Zechariah 8:21**] "The inhabitants of one city shall go to another, saying, 'Let us continue to go and pray before the Lord, and seek the Lord of hosts. I myself will go also." So join us there, let your friends know that you are going, and invite them to join you!

• Seek God's Prayer Plan for Your Life!

There are many levels of prayer

God knows exactly where each of us are in our prayer life and our knowledge and understanding of prayer.

He will honor even the most pitiful prayer a person offers in faith, if that is all they know to do. But He will not let us stay at that level.

He wants us to move to greater levels of understanding, faith, and power.

And the best way to progress is to simply say, "Lord, teach me to pray powerful and effective prayers."

Walking in the Supernatural Power of Prayer

Recommended Reading

1. Communion With God   by: Mark and Patti Virkler
2. Spirit Born Creativity   by: Mark Virkler
3. The Fourth Dimension II   by: David Young Cho
4. Hearing God   by: Peter Lord
5. Celebration of Discipline   by: Richard Foster
6. Communion With The Holy Spirit   by: Watchman Nee
7. Hear His Voice   by: Douglas Wead
8. Hearing His Voice   by: John Patrick Grace
9. The Way Into The Holiest   by: Derek Prince
10. The Soul's Sincere Desire   by: Glenn Clark
11. The Gentle Breeze Of Jesus   by: Mel and Nona Tari
12. Abide in Christ   by: Andrew Murray
13. God's Chosen Fast   by: Arthur Wallis
14. Whatever Happened to Hope   by: Dr. Roy Hicks
15. With Signs Following   by: Stanley H. Frodsham
16. Our Authority Over Sickness And The Devil   by: Gardner
17. The Two Covenants and the Second Blessing   by Andrew Murray
18. The Full Blessing of Pentecost   by Andrew Murray
19. Pentecostal Pioneers Remembered   by Keith Malcomson
20. The Prayer Ministry of the Church   by Watchman Nee
21. Gathered In His Name   by Watchman Nee
22. Man has been given power to make way for, or to obstruct the power of God   by Watchman Nee
23. Let the Lion Roar - Movie-Francoise Frank
24. Who Ate Lunch With Abraham - Rabbi Asher Intrater
25. Let Us Pray - Watchman Nee
26. Prayer and God's Work - Watchman Nee

Recommended Authors

Andrew Murray
David Young Cho
Watchman Nee
Derek Prince
Dr. Roy Hicks
Aimee Semple Mc Phearson
Stanley H. Frodsham
Leonard Ravenhill
David Ravenhill
David Wilkerson
Charles Spurgeon
Smith Wigglesworth
T.B. Barrett
A.A. Boddy
Cecil Polhill
Robert A Brown
Charles Spurgeon
W.J. Williams
John G. Lake
D.L. Moody
George Mueller
George Stormont
R.A. Torrey
William J Seymour
David Brenner
John Wesley
Charles & Frances Hunter
Kenneth Hagin Sr.

ABOUT THE AUTHOR

Dr. Henry Lewis and Patricia Lewis is the President and Co- President of an Apostolic International ministry called **Joshua International**. They have been married for 43 years and have two children and 6 grandchildren. Henry Lewis is a Sicilian Scottish Jew. His descendants come from Italy, Scotland and S Africa. Patricia is Canadian French, Native American and German. Descendants are traced from Canada, Paris, Switzerland, Russia, UK, Netherlands, Ireland and Germany.

Henry is a descendent of the famous Author and Pastor **Andrew Murray**. One of Andrew Murray's descendants were named after him who pastored in Fall River, MA

Dr. Lewis has authored 12 books which is still increasing. The first book called 'The Unholy Anointing' which later was changed to ' A Quest for Spiritual Power' is now translated in Arabic and in French. Over 7000 copies sold in Arabic. All books are sold on Amazon under H.A.Lewis.

Henry is a sought-after speaker and author, teaching at churches and conferences along with numerous TV guest media outlets teaching on subjects such as: spiritual warfare, revival, transformation, revelation, transforming prayer. Henry teaches amongst international prophetic leaders in many countries and holds three Doctorates in Counseling, Theology and Christian Education.

Charisma magazine shared his testimony as a former political occult leader in 2000. 750,000 Hindus accepted Christ after this article was translated in their language.

Henry's faith foundational friends are with : Dr. Leonard Heroo (Apostle and President of Zion Bible Institute & School of the Prophets), Evangelist Robert Schambach, Prophet David Wilkerson, Derek Prince, Lester Sumrall, Frank Hammond etc. Their passion and faith put a deep thirst for the knowledge and truth of God's word in them which resulted in having a deeper relationship with his Lord and Savior, Jesus Christ – and not a religion – so he could hear and know the voice of God.

Dr. Henry Lewis is ordained with the Assemblies of God. Henry is also ordained Rabbi through Asher Intrater from the Revive Israel Ministries

He is available for speaking

For More Information

Dr. H.A.Lewis
Joshua International

P.O. Box 1799
Maricopa, AZ 85139

Email: Info@halewis.org
Email: Info@ joshua-edu.org

To order or inquire of additional products, visit us online

Website: www.halewis.org
Visit us on face book

Book Cover Artist: Debbie Wheat
Contact: izayu54@yahoo.com

Book Co-coordinators

Grace Miller
Patricia Lewis

BOOKS

A Quest for Spiritual Power - Redeemed from the Curse - Testimonial
Choisi Par Le Maitre: En quête de puissance spirituelle - French translation
A Quest for Spiritual Power - Arabic translation
Nimrod - How religions began and how it applies today
Spiritual Opposition to the Five Fold Ministry
The Secret Names of the Strongmen - study material & prayer manual
Jezebel - human or the spirit of baal?
The Dispensation of the Lion and the lamb
The Return of the Days of Noah
The War between the Unseen Kingdoms

Available on Amazon

https://www.amazon.com/-/e/B01L7UBNDE

H.A.Lewis

www.ingramcontent.com/pod-product-compliance
Lightning Source LLC
LaVergne TN
LVHW081357060426
835510LV00016B/1876